graphic design for non-designers

Dedicated to Sarah, a nondesigner with a good eye for type

graphic design for non-designers

ESSENTIAL KNOWLEDGE, TIPS, AND TRICKS,
PLUS **20** STEP-BY-STEP PROJECTS FOR THE DESIGN NOVICE

BY TONY SEDDON & JANE WATERHOUSE
ILLUSTRATIONS BY RICK LANDERS

CHRONICLE BOOKS
SAN FRANCISCO

First published in the United States in 2009 by Chronicle Books LLC.

First published in the United Kingdom by RotoVision SA.

Copyright © 2009 by RotoVision SA.

Library of Congress Cataloging-in-Publication Data available.

ISBN: 978-0-8118-6831-0

Manufactured in China.
Design and Art Direction: Tony Seddon and Jane Waterhouse

Cover design by Allison Weiner

10 9 8 7 6 5 4 3 2 1

Chronicle Books LLC
680 Second Street
San Francisco, CA 94107

www.chroniclebooks.com

Contents

Introduction

If you have bought this book, or even received it as a gift (lucky you!), then presumably, you have at least a passing interest in graphic design. You've probably thought at some stage or other that it would be great if you could design a new business card for yourself, or perhaps that you would love to design the invitation for a friend's wedding, but you don't know where to start. Well, we're here to help you out with that.

When I first mentioned to a couple of friends, who also happen to be graphic design professionals (we're an incestuous lot you know), that Jane and I were writing and designing a book to teach design rookies how to put together their own design projects, they raised their eyebrows and asked, "What are you trying to do? Put us out of business!"

The answer is, of course, not at all. It takes years of study and practice to become a professional graphic designer with the expertise to warrant commercial rates for your services, and there is no book I've seen on the subject which can achieve that in 224 pages. What this book can do, however, is furnish you with many of the basic theories and tools of the trade that graphic designers use every day to create stationery, newsletters, posters, brochures, logos, and so on.

The first half of the book covers equipment and materials; the techniques that control the use of space and structure in layouts; the use of photography, illustration, color, and type; and the preparation of artwork for printing by a professional printing firm.

The second half consists of 20 typical projects that you might want to tackle yourselves, either because you simply want to have a go at some graphic design, or because you are not in a position to budget for the services of a professional designer. The topics discussed throughout will arm you with the knowledge you need to tackle projects with confidence, and, with some practice and experimentation, you'll be better placed to create more successful and professional-looking pieces of graphic design.

I started writing with the intention of keeping the book as computer-free as possible in order to accommodate those of you who don't have access to any relevant software packages. Pretty much everyone has a computer these days, but they don't necessarily own image-editing or layout software. It's a fact that most of the subjects discussed in the first half of the book are not at all reliant on available design software technology—they are about space, structure, color, and so on. However, it wasn't long before I realized that graphic design and computers are now inextricably linked. I should have realized this from the outset, considering the fact that the first thing I do on an average working day is switch on my computer, and the last thing I do before heading home is switch it off. Therefore, the discussions do, at times, rely on the assumption that you own a computer and that you have, at the very least, some knowledge of software that will allow you to edit a digital image or set a line of type. This could be anything from Adobe Photoshop or InDesign down to the most basic word-processing package, as either option can be used to create great-looking graphic design.

All that remains to say, before you head off into the book and begin to learn about the wonderful world of graphic design, is, don't be too concerned or get frustrated about the way your efforts turn out the first time around. All you need is a little patience and imagination and you'll be fine. We hope you enjoy what follows.

Tony Seddon and Jane Waterhouse

1

Getting Started

Terminology

Graphic design terminology is covered in detail in the Graphic Design Jargon Buster on pages 202–209, but here are a few of the more common terms used throughout this book.

ascender: the portion of a lowercase letter that sits above the x-height, as for b, d, and k.

baseline grid: a series of horizontal divisions, normally measured in points, upon which successive rows of type sit. Using a baseline grid helps with the alignment of lines of text across columns in a page layout.

CMYK: the abbreviation for cyan, magenta, yellow, and black, the colors used in the four-color printing process.

crop/cropping: when you cut off areas of an image to zoom in on a detail, you are cropping that image.

descender: the portion of a lowercase letter that sits below the baseline, as for g, q, and p.

DPI (dots per inch): the resolution of an image once it is printed is measured in dots per inch. Optimum print quality is achieved with a 300ppi (*see* PPI) image reproduced at actual size or smaller.

font: another word for typeface, or more specifically a particular weight (e.g., bold) or size from a larger typeface family.

four-color process: color printing using the three primary colors of cyan, magenta, and yellow, plus black. Images must first be broken down into minute halftone dots of varying sizes and combinations; when combined these produce the full range of printed colors.

graphic: a generic term used to describe an individual element in a design (e.g. an imported logo or diagram, or a colored panel).

gsm or g/m^2: the abbreviation for grams per square meter, which is used to describe the weight and therefore thickness of paper.

halftone: a photograph that has been screened so it can be reproduced as a series of dots using the four-color printing process.

header/headline: a large piece of type at the top of a page, indicating the main subject being discussed.

hue: the main attribute of a color, e.g., its redness or blueness, rather than its shade or saturation.

layout: the overall arrangement of a piece of design (e.g. a page from a magazine).

lightbox: a suitcase-sized, glass-topped, backlit light source used for tracing reference material, or for viewing color transparencies or slides. A light table is easy to make at home using a sheet of thick glass or Perspex balanced on trestles, with an ordinary desk lamp placed beneath it.

point size: type is measured in points, and its size referred to as its point size. One point is approximately 0.35mm (0.014in). Rule thickness is also defined using points.

ppi (pixels per inch): image resolution is measured in pixels per inch. The higher the ppi, the larger the image can be printed. The optimum resolution for a good-quality print is 300ppi.

RGB: the abbreviation for red, green, and blue, the three additive colors used to create an image on a monitor, or a digital photo.

rule: a single straight line. The width, or weight, of a rule is often specified in points, but can also be given in millimeters or inches.

sans serif: the generic term for a font that doesn't feature small extensions at the end of the strokes, one of the best-known examples being *Helvetica*.

serif: the generic term for a font that does feature small extensions at the end of the strokes, *and* the short extensions themselves. Garamond is an example of a serif font.

stock: when professional designers or printers refer to the type of paper or board specified for a print project, they call it the stock.

tint: a shade or variation of color, specified as a percentage of a solid ink color. The term can also describe an area of printed color in a layout.

transparency: an alternative name for a photographic image shot on slide film.

vector: graphics that use points, lines, curves, and polygons to form the image. Mathematical equations calculate the position and size of the points and shapes, which means that vector images can be reproduced at any size without any loss of quality. Logos are a good example of a popular use for vector graphics.

Equipment

If you were asked to name the single most important tool for creating graphic design, your answer would probably be "a computer." That's a fair response, and we'll talk about computers later, but first of all, it's really important to get yourself some pencils or markers and a layout pad to sketch up some ideas. Computers capable of producing the kind of graphic design that surrounds us today began to appear in the late 1980s which, relatively speaking, isn't so long ago. Prior to that all graphic design concepts were realized through hand-drawn visuals, and the majority of professional designers still reach for a pencil before a mouse when forming new ideas.

I find it more difficult to conceive ideas directly on a computer. To really get the ideas flowing, I think the best thing you can do is doodle on a sheet of paper. You won't be limited by your computer skills, you won't be tempted to go for boring solutions that the computer can create for you "out of the box," and you'll be able to dedicate your entire thought process to coming up with ideas. You don't have to be able to draw like an accomplished artist to do this. Visuals are snapshots of developing ideas—they don't have to look like finished pieces of graphic design.

Buying choices & budget

Try to buy the best-quality tools and equipment you can afford. My father, an engineer, always advised me never to buy a cheap wrench as it would eventually let me down. This can also be said of felt-tip pens and layout or tracing pads. Poor-quality markers used on poor-quality paper produce poor-quality marks, which could ruin an otherwise well-conceived visual. If you have any local suppliers specializing in graphics materials, ask their advice about the best tools for your planned projects, and always compare the online prices of any equipment you want before you hand over your hard-earned cash.

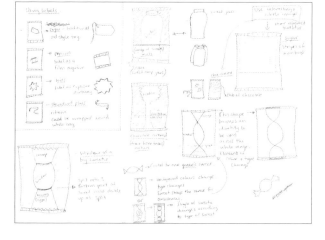

← Despite the wonders of today's design software, there is still no substitute for pencils and paper when formulating new ideas. Grab yourself a few sheets of plain paper and get all those ideas down in rough form before you spend a lot of time working on something that might turn out not to be the best solution for your project.

Markers

There are dozens of brands available, so do a bit of research and, if possible, buy single markers in order to try them out before you buy a whole pack. Good suppliers should have samplers of the main brands for you to try before you commit to a purchase.

Graphic markers are often referred to generically as magic markers, but Magic Marker is also the brand name of what is arguably the most popular choice of design professionals. The quality of these markers is second to none, and they are conveniently supplied with both chisel- and fine-tip ends, but be aware that they are at the expensive end of the price range. An alternative that I like, despite its relatively limited range of available colors, is Sharpie markers. Sharpie is a classic brand whose products are affordable, good for general everyday tasks, keep their points really well, and don't run dry quickly.

↑ ↑ *Royal Sovereign Magic Markers are widely available from good graphic supplies stores and online, and are of the highest quality. They're not cheap, but you do get what you pay for.*

↑ *I love Sharpie Fine Point permanent markers for everyday doodling, and for hand-lettering. They are reasonably priced, very hardwearing, and able to write on lots of different surfaces.*

In addition to the type and width of a pen's tip, the thickness of the barrel affects how comfortable and flexible it is in use. I like fairly chunky pens for sketching out rough ideas as you can hold the pen in a greater number of ways in order to achieve a more varied range of line weights and stroke shapes. For more detailed drawing, or for ruling out lines, I prefer a slimmer, fine-line pen which doesn't obscure the point at which the pen's tip meets the paper. For these you can't go wrong with any of the superb products from either Pilot or uni-ball. Both brands offer a huge range of affordable products to meet every need.

Layout & tracing pads

Layout pads might seem like an unnecessary extravagance, but the crisp white paper in a decent-quality layout pad allows markers to produce cleaner strokes, and your visuals will look better for it. Furthermore, your marker pens won't dry out so quickly because layout paper isn't overly absorbent. If you need to copy the outlines of a reference image, a tracing pad will make life much easier, but if you don't want to stretch to the extra expense you can use cheap wax (greaseproof) paper from the kitchen cupboard. Lightweight layout paper can also double up as trace if the details you need to copy aren't too fine, particularly if you use a lightbox.

← *Learning how to make different types of mark with your collection of pens and pencils will pay dividends when you begin to visualize your ideas. Spend time practicing on loose sheets of paper in order to perfect your mark-making skills.*

← You may want to consider purchasing an inexpensive magnifier, or loupe for checking small details in transparencies when using a lightbox.

↑ A professional lightbox like the one shown here has a light source that is color-corrected to allow accurate color display and a very even dispersal of light across the entire surface of the glass. They are relatively expensive, but cheaper options with standard bulbs are readily available. Alternatively, you can make your own with a sheet of glass or stiff Perspex and a desk lamp. This solution is perfectly acceptable for tracing outlines from found reference material.

Tapes & adhesives

The minimum you're likely to need is a roll of masking tape for general use, a roll of invisible tape for applications that require a neater finish, and a can of 3M SprayMount™ for mounting paper or card. There are several different types of spray adhesive produced by 3M, but SprayMount™ Repositionable Adhesive (the one in the blue can) is the most versatile for general artworking requirements. You can reposition artwork that's not set perfectly in place, and paper or card won't wrinkle after you've applied the adhesive. Always use SprayMount™ in a well-ventilated area, and make sure you read the instructions and advice on how to use the product correctly.

Scalpels & cutting mats

A craft knife is OK for basic cutting and trimming needs, but a good-quality scalpel with a sharp new blade will produce a cut of, forgive the pun, surgical precision. Dahle and Swann-Morton are good brands of surgical-type scalpels, and X-ACTO make excellent precision knives for fine cutting work. If your budget is limited you can cut on a spare piece of thick card, but a plastic, self-healing cutting mat is a much better option and will last for years. You must take care when using these very sharp tools; make sure you read more about cutting techniques on pages 026–029.

Steel rules

All you need is a cheap steel rule from your local hardware store. An absolutely vital piece of advice is never to cut with a plastic rule: the blade can easily skip off its edge. At best the cut won't be straight; at worst you could suffer a serious injury.

↑ *A collection of various types of adhesive tape is essential if you plan to make any packs, booklets, or brochures by hand. As well as a standard roll of Scotch tape, get some masking tape for general tasks, and a roll of invisible tape. Invisible tape, being low-tack, is therefore also removable. Finally, a roll of double-sided tape will prove to be invaluable.*

← *3M produces four varieties of adhesive, of which SprayMount is the most versatile. It provides a secure bond, but allows repositioning if necessary. DisplayMount bonds both nonporous and porous surfaces; ReMount forms a nonpermanent, low-tack bond; and PhotoMount creates a heavy-duty, permanent bond.*

↑ ↑ A self-healing
cutting mat provides
a cutting surface that is
much better than a piece
of card, or the surface of
your desk! Your cuts will
be cleaner, and your
blade less likely to slip.

↑ There are a number of
options for precise cutting
of paper and card. One of
the best and most cost-
effective tools is a surgical
scalpel. These are better
than the plastic-handled
craft knives, but take care
when fitting new blades
(see page 027).

→ An inexpensive steel
rule from your local
hardware store will
serve you well.

Paper

One of the most important decisions a professional graphic designer has to make when working on a print project is which paper to use. The type of paper you choose for your own projects will play a significant role in their look and feel, so it is worth having an idea of the various types available to you. Paper stock is categorized as either coated, which has a smooth surface and is better for printing color; or uncoated, which has a more textured surface, and is generally more absorbent, so colors printed on it tend to appear less vibrant.

Copy paper

This relatively cheap paper is usually uncoated and of basic quality, but with a fairly smooth surface, and is normally around 80gsm in weight. (A paper's weight gives an indication of its thickness.) Copy paper is perfect for printing low-coverage text or for photocopying, but it is quite absorbent so tends to wrinkle when large areas of wet ink are applied, and will not give good results if used in an inkjet to print color photographs or layouts with lots of color tints. Generally speaking, the higher the gsm, the thicker the paper will be, and the less likely it will be to wrinkle during printing.

Inkjet paper

Inkjet paper is made specifically for use in inkjet printers, is available in a wide range of weights, and is of a higher quality than standard copy paper. This quality sets inkjet paper apart from other types of mid-weight paper stock. It is usually coated with either a matte or glossy finish, which means it isn't as absorbent as the cheaper alternatives. This helps to prevent wrinkling and allows the surface of the paper to accept finer print details. I strongly recommend that you use a good-quality inkjet paper to output your own projects as the final results will look a lot better for it.

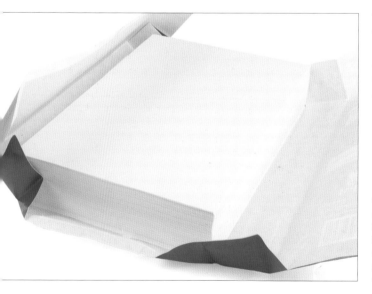

← *Copy paper is good for everyday use. Don't expect the best results if you print full-color photos on an inkjet, however, as the paper's absorbency will ruin the color vibrancy.*

Photo paper

If you want to print great-looking photos through your inkjet printer, photo paper is an absolute must. As with inkjet paper, there are lots of weights and finishes from which to choose, but in general it's a sound option to go for a glossy finish when printing bright, colorful images, and a matte (or uncoated) finish for moody black-and-white shots. Photo paper can be more expensive again, but the results make the extra cost well worth it.

There are literally thousands of finishes and colors of paper stock available, far too many to talk about here, so do a bit of your own research and try to be adventurous with your choices.

↑ You don't have to stick to white paper. There are thousands of shades and textures of colored paper suitable for use in inkjet printers and photocopiers.

← These examples indicate how an image will appear when output on cheap copy paper (far left) and photo paper (left). Note how the colors are more muted on the lower-quality paper, and how the details are less well defined.

Computers

I would be happy to bet you have a computer in your home or office that you could use right now for your graphic design projects. Many professional designers use Apple products and will tell you they're the only brand suitable for running design applications. It's true they're wonderful machines—personally I've never used any other kind—but good-quality PCs with a decent specification and the right software are perfectly capable graphic design workstations.

You really don't have to use a computer to produce graphic design, but they're undoubtedly a very useful addition to your graphic design toolbox. The great thing about using computers for graphic design is that they can produce effects which you can't achieve using your hand-rendering skills alone. However, they don't come up with the ideas for you (at least not yet anyway), so don't be fooled into thinking they're the easy option. Think of them as an expensive marker that you have to plug in!

Choosing a computer

I'm going to offer you the same advice here as I did for pens and layout pads: a poor-quality computer will give poor service, so decide on your budget and go for the best possible machine that you can afford. In my experience, if your chosen manufacturer offers several build options for each model, the middle

→ *The range of desktop and laptop computers available from Apple covers every possible need of the professional and nonprofessional creative. They are marvelous machines with a very high specification, and,* *at the lower end of the range, prices are not as high as you might expect. This model is of the highly regarded MacBook.* **Courtesy of Apple.**

MacBook

option is likely to offer the best combination of performance and value for money. Having said that, don't be tempted to pay out heaps of cash for a machine that's more powerful than you need it to be. If the cost difference between two models is minimal, it's probably a good idea to stretch your budget and go for the higher specification, but find out why the more expensive model is worth the extra cost and then decide if you really need that extra performance or not.

Think about your working space as well. If you're lucky enough to have a dedicated workspace, a desktop model might be right for you; if not, a laptop is a great option, particularly as they're now comparable in performance to desktop machines. Finally, don't be tempted to go for a brand that doesn't offer watertight after-sales service which covers both hardware and software support.

⬇ All-in-one desktop machines, like the Dell XPS One PC, offer a great solution for people who need the power of a desktop machine, but have only a limited amount of workspace available.
Courtesy of Dell Inc.

Software

If you're really serious about graphic design, there are some really serious software packages to consider. Be aware that professional design software is highly sophisticated, with lots of features, so the average learning curve is quite steep, especially if you're trying to get your head around basic graphic design principles at the same time.

↑ *The user interface of Adobe's Photoshop Elements is extremely easy to master, with lots of built-in functions that do all the complicated work for you.*

Professional design software

Adobe's Creative Suite family [www.adobe.com] is extremely popular with design professionals, particularly because Photoshop is part of the package. Photoshop is *the* image-editing application of choice—so much so that digitally altered or enhanced images are often automatically referred to as Photoshopped images. If you can afford only one design application, Photoshop is probably the one you can achieve most with, as its typographic functions are also very sophisticated. There's a much cheaper option too—Photoshop Elements. This has loads of great, easy-to-use features that make complex image-editing tasks a breeze.

Photoshop only creates single-page documents, so for multipage layout work the professional choice is either InDesign, part of the Adobe Creative Suite, or QuarkXPress [www.quark.com], which was one of the applications responsible for the success of the original desktop publishing (DTP) revolution. These DTP applications are essentially highly evolved word processors that can produce very sophisticated layouts with all text, images, and graphics in place. The book you're reading was designed using InDesign CS3.

Unfortunately, professional design software doesn't come cheap, so unless you've got money to burn, deciding to purchase an application is a big decision. It's normally possible to download a trial version of your chosen application; this will run for a limited period so that you can evaluate it and decide if you want to buy. I highly recommend this.

Word processors

The alternative is the word-processing software which everyone has on their PC or Mac. For PC owners running Windows this is probably going to be Word; for Mac owners it may be either Word or Pages '08 from the iWork '08 software package. There are lots of alternatives of course, too numerous to mention here, but the point is that this software is easy to use and much cheaper than the professional applications. There's no reason at all why you can't use your basic word processor to produce sophisticated pieces of graphic design, either as documents constructed entirely on screen, or by printing out and assembling material using traditional cut-and-paste methods. The principles we cover on the following spreads can be applied regardless of what software you have available.

Software piracy

As tempting as it may seem, please don't download pirated software. Apart from the obvious fact that it's against the law, you won't get any of the benefits provided for registered owners, such as online support and tutorials. These are important extras for design novices as they'll help you get up to speed quickly.

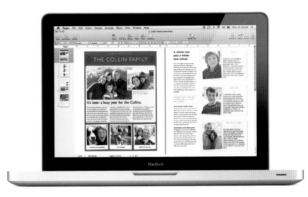

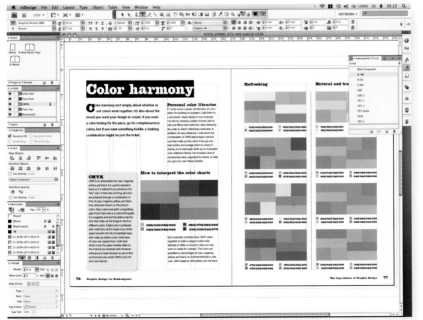

↑ Pages '09, part of Apple's inexpensive iWork '09 suite, is a powerful word processor capable of producing complex layouts.
Courtesy of Apple.

← This page was laid out using InDesign from Adobe. It is the layout software of choice for many professional designers. While it isn't simple software to master, it is extremely powerful and very highly featured. If you plan to take your design work further, this is one piece of software you should take a look at.

Cut, crease, fold

A professional finish will add to the success of your projects. Cutting and folding are important skills to master—a clean cut and correct fold make all the difference to a finished piece—and it's even more important to learn how to cut safely.

X-ACTO knives & surgical scalpels

A good-quality pair of scissors is an important part of the graphic designer's toolkit. However, if you want to produce a clean, accurate cut through a sheet of paper or card, an X-ACTO knife or surgical scalpel will serve you much better. These high-quality, but inexpensive cutting tools can be purchased from any regular graphic arts supplier, with the handles and blades sold separately. If you're under 16 you may be under the legal age to buy a product like this yourself.

The most popular combination of handle and blade among professional designers is a size 1 X-ACTO handle with a size 11 blade, or if you' re using a surgical scalpel, a size 3 handle with a 10A blade. Other useful scalpel blades to consider are a number 10 which has a round profile (I find this type useful for cutting freehand curves), and a number 11 which is slightly more pointed than a 10A, making it good for intricate cutting work.

→ X-ACTO have been making precision tools for artists and graphic designers for over 75 years, and the brand name is synonymous with all cutting requirements.

→ A soft-drink can is ideal for making a sharps bin for used scalpel blades: the small hole in the top prevents items from falling out easily when the can is discarded.

The first thing to learn is how to fit a new blade to a handle. It's important to change blades often as worn blades won't produce a good, clean cut: swap the used blade for a new one between projects. To fit a new blade, push it carefully to halfway down the narrow slotted end of the handle, holding it by its blunt edge. **1**

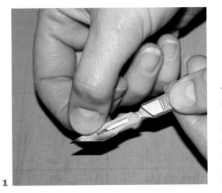

Next, gently push the pointed end of the blade against a flat surface that you don't mind marking, or better still into your cutting mat. The blade will snap easily onto the handle without your fingers getting near the sharp edge. To remove a used blade, gently lift the back of the blade away from its mounting and carefully push it forward off the handle. Don't throw used blades into your waste basket where they could later cause an injury. Make a "sharps" bin out of a used metal drinks can and dispose of it safely once it's full. **2**

Sharps bins are bins used to dispose of sharp implements safely. The term comes from the medical profession.

3

← *Great care must be taken when fitting and removing scalpel or craft-knife blades. Keep your fingers away from the sharp side of the blade when handling it (1), and never use your fingers to push the blade onto the handle. Apply pressure by pressing the tip of the blade into a cutting mat or thick card surface (2) until it slips onto the handle correctly. When removing the blade, push from the back first (3), remembering to keep your fingers away from the sharp edge.*

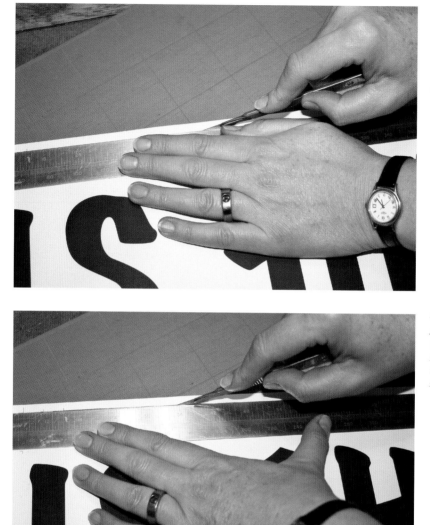

← How not to cut using a scalpel and steel rule! Your fingers should be behind the cutting edge, and your scalpel should be at a right angle to the surface you are cutting.

← How it should be done. All fingertips are clear of the rule's edge, and the scalpel is upright and therefore less likely to slip and cause injury.

If you're cutting along a straightedge, always use a steel or steel-edged rule, never a plastic one: the sharp scalpel will cut into the plastic rule, and could easily slip toward your fingers, giving you a nasty cut. I witnessed a colleague take the tip of his left index finger off with a scalpel once when cutting with a plastic rule. Be warned, it's not a pleasant experience! Hold the rule firmly with your index and middle fingers and thumb, taking care to keep them away from the rule's edge, and run the scalpel gently down the edge toward you. The scalpel, if it is sharp, should cut through paper easily with one stroke. If you're cutting thicker paper or card, don't try to cut through in one pass. Run the scalpel along the rule's edge several times, cutting a little deeper with each pass, until you're all the way through. The cut will be much cleaner if you follow this method, and it's much easier as less pressure is required.

I've one more cutting tip for you— always cover the area you want to keep with the rule, with the paper you plan to discard visible. This way, if you happen to accidentally move the scalpel blade away from the edge of the rule, you'll not be cutting into your artwork.

Successful folding

If you want to create a very precise fold along a particular line, there's a very simple trick. Set your steel rule along the line that you want to fold, and *score* an indented line along the full length of the fold. I tend to use the rounded end of my scalpel handle to do this: it's perfect for scoring card which would otherwise not fold easily, and the brass handle doesn't mark the card's surface. Be careful not to stick the blade into the palm of your hand though! For very precise scoring you can even use the scalpel blade itself, turned upward so the sharp edge is pointing away from the paper surface, but only exert a tiny amount of pressure or you'll cut through rather than score. The paper stock will fold easily once your scored line is in place.

← The example shown far left is the result of card being folded without any scoring. The fold is not precise, and the card has been torn slightly where the tension has pulled the fibers apart. The near example was scored along the back of the fold with the blunt edge of a scalpel blade, producing a much neater fold with few or no stress tears.

Sourcing images

There's a simple choice to make when you need an image for one of your graphic design projects—do you create it yourself, or do you use one that someone else has created? If you're not an accomplished photographer you could be forgiven for opting to go with the latter, but if you don't have a go yourself how will you ever discover that latent talent waiting to burst out?

Taking your own photographs

Before the advent of digital cameras it wasn't easy to produce photographic images in a form that you could easily use for a graphic design project without specialist knowledge and equipment. For most of us the only option available was the nearest photo lab where your exposed film could be processed and printed—at considerable expense if you needed a nonstandard print. Added to that, the skills then needed to take the prints and combine them with type and other imagery in a graphics project were not available to most nonprofessionals. However, now that we have digital cameras, everything has changed. For a relatively small outlay you can buy a consumer-level digital camera capable of capturing images of a very high quality. Advances in camera technology mean that even compact digital cameras are now able to produce images that will look great when output at large size from an inkjet printer. Many of you will already own a digital camera of some kind, but if you're thinking of an upgrade, or if you're looking to make your first purchase, there are some basic points to consider.

← Before you use your digital camera, read the section of your manual that covers how you should hold it. This is more important than you may think, and your images will be sharper, with less "camera shake," if you get this right.

Choosing & buying a camera

Your first consideration when choosing which camera to go for will probably be based on your budget. In the past, compact cameras (unless they had a very high specification) were generally cheaper than SLRs. However, there are now many competitively priced SLRs coming to the market. Just take a look at any camera retailer's website and check out the great deals available. This means you can base your choice on a broader range of criteria, namely how and where you plan to use the camera, and what kind of pictures you want to take.

↓ The Canon IXUS 870 IS, a 10-megapixel compact camera, is capable of producing high-quality images suitable for use in your design projects. Courtesy of Canon.

← The Nikon D90 is a versatile 12.3-megapixel SLR at the top of the company's range of consumer digital SLRs. A camera of this quality will cope with a vast array of photographic situations, not least because the lens is inter-changeable with other Nikon lenses. It is an ideal choice for anyone serious about photography for use in their design projects. Courtesy of Nikon.

Compacts

Compact cameras are very convenient because of their size, and they're often easier to use than SLR cameras because of the wealth of automatic features available on most models. They're ideal for everyday photography as you can carry them with you in your bag or pocket, meaning you never miss an opportunity to grab an interesting shot that you could use in a project. Indeed, many professional photographers and designers carry a compact with them all the time for this very reason. However, compacts do have some limitations which you should consider. Firstly, they're not as good for flash photography because the lens and flash are so close together. This is why you often see the red-eye effect in portraits taken with

a compact—light from the flash bounces off the subject's eyes straight back into the lens. Secondly, the smaller digital sensors used in most compacts produce slightly grainier (noisier) images than an SLR, and that digital noise will be visible in enlarged photographic prints. Thirdly, and in my opinion the biggest drawback, is the fact that the lenses aren't interchangeable and are often fixed-focus with a limited zoom range. Don't be fooled by cameras that boast a large digital zoom. All this does is enlarge a portion of the scene you're looking at in the viewfinder, meaning that image quality is compromised. Look at the optical zoom range when choosing your camera, as this is what really counts in terms of camera performance.

↑ Compacts tend to rely on LCD screens on the back of the camera for framing shots, but it's useful to have the option of an optical viewfinder, as with the IXUS 980 IS from Canon. Viewfinders are useful for achieving more accurate framing, and for bright days when sunshine reflects off the LCD screen, making it difficult to view.
Courtesy of Canon.

← The rather scary effect known as "red eye" is caused by light from a built-in flash bouncing straight back into the camera lens. Compacts are prone to this; use the built-in red-eye reduction facility when you shoot portraits, if your model has this feature.
Photography © Tony Seddon

← ↑ Digital noise is caused by random pixels of light scattered throughout a digitally shot image. The relatively large amounts of amplification needed for images shot with the smaller CCD sensors in compacts can cause this effect, as can the slow shutter speeds needed for images shot in low-light conditions.
Photography © Tony Seddon

SLRs

There are no two ways about this. A photo taken with an SLR will be of a better overall quality than one taken using a compact. The excuse for not opting for an SLR is often that "They're complicated to use and I don't know anything about cameras." Well, SLRs have got an auto setting too, so if you only ever use that setting you won't need to learn anything about aperture and shutter-speed settings. That would be a shame though, as a little knowledge of these things will produce exciting images that will greatly enhance your design projects.

There are some great books available that will teach you how to use your shiny new SLR, so I won't go into all that here. Other big advantages of SLRs over compacts are that they're much faster to power up, focus, and write to the internal memory card. This means that you're less likely to miss a shot, particularly if it's an action shot of a fast-moving object. Secondly, they're much more flexible for all sorts of varying lighting conditions. You have the choice to have complete control over the settings with an SLR so you can make images that a compact would never be able to capture. Thirdly, you have a choice of literally dozens of different lenses, providing you with greater control over the type of image you can capture (for e.g., wide-angle lenses are useful for photographing in cramped interiors, and telephoto lenses for shooting distant objects).

The ideal is to be a little indulgent and have both a compact and an SLR at your disposal which, given the bargains that can be found if you shop around, isn't too much of a stretch. Considering the fact that your primary need for most design projects will be high-quality images that can be enlarged as much as possible, my personal recommendation would be a good-quality SLR rated at 8 megapixels or higher, and a mid-range (and therefore cheaper) compact, with as high a megapixel rating as you can find along with a decent set of built-in features. As with all equipment, go for the best that you can afford and you won't be disappointed.

→ *The 18–70mm, f/3.5–4.5G ED-IF AF-S DX Zoom Nikkor lens. A lens of this type and specification is suitable for a very wide range of situations, from landscapes to portraits and close-ups.*
Courtesy of Nikon.

← A universal USB 2.0 card reader from LaCie. These small, inexpensive input devices will accept a variety of formats, so are particularly useful if you have two cameras that use different types of card. *Courtesy of LaCie.*

↑ The back of the Nikon D90. A well-designed camera such as this allows easy and intuitive access to all the controls, and has a generously sized LCD screen for previewing your shots before downloading them to a computer. *Courtesy of Nikon.*

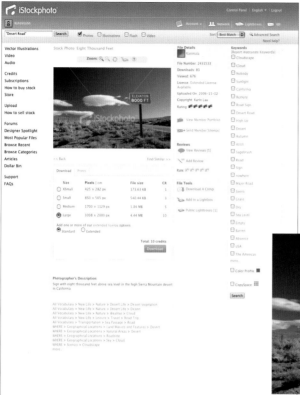

Online image libraries

Image libraries, or stock photography agencies to give them another name, have existed for many years, and their increased accessibility, provided by the Internet, has cemented their position as a major provider of photographic and illustrative imagery for professional designers. On the back of this we have seen the emergence of *microstock* libraries, which sell stock photography and illustration exclusively online, and offer images at very reasonable prices. There is a sliding scale of fees according to the size of the image bought, and how it will be used.

↑ *This picture from the iStockphoto image library is offered at four sizes/resolutions, at a range of corresponding prices. If you're sure you'll only need the smallest version of the picture, don't spend more cash than you need to, but if you think you may need a larger version of the image in the future, invest in the larger size from the outset.*
www.istockphoto.com

Megapixel ratings explained

The resolution at which a camera captures images is determined by its megapixel rating. As the relationship between ratings and physical image dimensions can be confusing, we've compiled this guide to the maximum dimensions at which you can expect to produce a good-quality print, based on the megapixel rating of your camera.

Maximum print size (cm/in)	Minimum rating (megapixels)	Resolution (ppi)
10 × 15/4 × 6	2	1,600 × 1,200
13 × 18/5 × 7	3	2,048 × 1,536
20 × 25/8 × 10	5	2,560 × 1,920
28 × 36/11 × 14	6	2,816 × 2,112
41 × 51/16 × 20	8	3,264 × 2,468

The prices vary between libraries, so do shop around for the best deals. The huge choice and great value provided by these image libraries mean that nonprofessional designers can easily source high-quality images for their own personal graphic design projects with just a few clicks of the mouse, and without having to spend a fortune. The large agencies that serve the graphics industry sell images on a *rights-managed* basis, meaning that a single-use license for the image is granted. You won't own the image you've paid for, just the right to use it as you specify in your purchase order. The initial usage fee is normally relatively high, and if you want to use the image again for another project an additional fee must be paid. Obviously, this can get quite expensive, and isn't really suitable for the average self-initiated graphic design project. Images sold through the microstock libraries, however, are *royalty-free* which means that, for a one-off payment, they can be used as many times and in as many ways as you choose. This is a much more practical proposition for the nondesigner operating on a small budget. Some royalty-free libraries also offer subscription deals where you can pay a set fee monthly or annually for a given number of daily downloads—useful if you're regularly sourcing lots of images.

We've listed a number of image library sites in the Online image resources directory section (*see* pages 217–219).

→ *Flickr (www.flickr.com) is not an image library; it is an online community that allows people to share their photographs with other photographers. It is not for commercial purposes, and selling images through the site is not permitted. However, it is a great place to see what other people are shooting, and is an* extremely inspiring site to visit. This page shows the work of Steve Luck, who was happy for us to feature his work here. Never download another person's images unless you have requested, and received, their permission to do so.

Courtesy of Flickr and Yahoo.

Image size

If the library you purchase from offers a choice of image size, and if the image will be yours to use again in the future, think about buying the largest size available, even if it's larger than your immediate needs—you may want to use it at a larger size the next time. For the sake of a few dollars it could be a good investment.

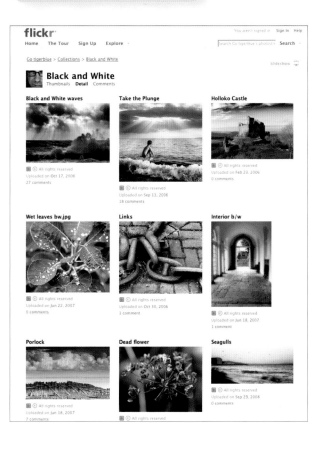

Copyright©

There is a commonly held belief that copyright has to be registered in some way, like a patent. This is not entirely true as copyright is automatically assigned to any piece of work that is created in physical form, and no publication or registration through official channels is required to secure copyright. It is therefore important to always respect this fact when searching through existing material to use in your own design projects.

It is possible to formally register copyright if the creator wishes, and a public record of copyright on a piece of work could provide obvious advantages to its creator if a dispute over usage occurred. However, many professional graphic designers and photographers do not go to the trouble and expense of registering every piece of work they create, and there's no reason why they should feel they have to under the standard rules of copyright protection.

Copyright must be adhered to at all times, and the bottom line is that without the copyright holder's permission, you cannot and should not use someone else's copyright-protected material in any of your projects. Many of your personal projects are likely to be experimental or noncommercial, but it's still important to be respectful of the originator's copyright, particularly when it comes to images that you find through the Internet. If you do want to use material you've come across online or elsewhere, but don't have the budget available for it, the owner of the copyright might be happy for you to use that material for a reduced fee, or even free of charge, depending on what you want to do with it. Contact the copyright holder and ask for their permission—the worst they can do is say no.

←→ *All these images are of the same physical object, but neither photographer can exercise any right over the other, even if the images have been shot from almost exactly the same position and angle.*

Creative Commons

Creative Commons is a relatively new approach to copyright. Conceived in 2001, it provides a platform for people who are happy for their work to be used for nonprofit or educational projects free of charge, as long as the work is credited to them. It basically offers the alternative "Some Rights Reserved" as opposed to the normal "All Rights Reserved" terms of traditional copyright. There are several alternative licenses that provide different permissible levels of usage; take a look at the Creative Commons website at www. creativecommons.org to find out more.

↑ A Creative Commons license enables people who want to share their work in specific ways to do so more easily without losing the ownership and rights of the original piece, where "some rights" rather than "all rights" are reserved.

2

Space & Structure

Using space

A layout is made up of many different elements: type, images, lines, circles, squares. However, every layout starts out as nothing more than open space—a challenge for nondesigners and professionals alike. If you think of *nonspace* elements as simple geometric objects, the layout can be broken down to the relationships between those elements and the space that surrounds them. Working successfully with this relationship sits at the very heart of good graphic design.

White space

Firstly we'll talk about what professional designers refer to as white space. This is space that isn't occupied by any type of graphic element, with the *white* referring to blank paper. Newcomers to graphic design tend to feel a little uneasy about white space, seeing it as a wasted opportunity when a couple more pictures or a bit more text can be squeezed in. Experienced designers use white space as an integral part of a layout, serving two main purposes.

The first is to provide a frame for objects or groups. This helps set them apart from the other elements of a layout which, in turn, produces better organization and visual clarity. The second is to help create better visual navigation or flow (*see* pages 054–055), by drawing the eye through a layout in the sequence you desire, or to the focal point of the layout. You could liken this to the way a garden designer might draw your eye toward a spectacular view by using an avenue of trees, or to put it another way, by using the space between the trees.

Don't be frightened of white space. It's a very important and useful component of the graphic design toolkit. When used correctly and creatively, it will help deliver a professional finish to your graphic design projects.

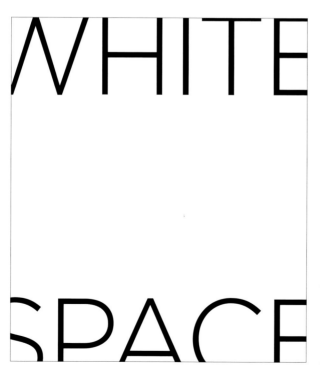

← *In this example do you read the text first, or do you see the white space and instantly know what the type says, just by association? This layout is pretty much all white space, but nonetheless* *it's a very effective piece of graphic design. It's also interesting to see how the words are clearly readable despite the fact that several of the characters are partly obscured.*

**Urerit, con utpat autat.
Duipsumsan hendip
endre velis nos dolore
dio commy nibh exero
core do elendip el
utpat. Duis niam, quat
uer summy nullutpat et,
summy nosto dolore.**

Urerit, con utpat autat. Duipsumsan hendip endre velis nos dolore dio commy nibh exero core do elendip el utpat. Duis niam, quatuer summy nullutpat et, summy nosto dolore consenit vel utem doluptat ut luptat doloborpero erat ver sit nis num volorerilit alit adignit lor sequat. Gue et lortisi sciliquam, sit nullum quis at. Dui tiscidunt laore doluptat wisci blam zzriurem accumsandre faciliquat iriusto core min vent enim dolenibh etum vero odo del iril irit dolobortis nullum volorpe

rilluptat nosto elisim volorer iureet ad tatio dolortin ullam venim venisi. Aci ex ex ea autpatisis alit velisl utem iustinim dunt iriliquis dolore magnim aci et del ulla autatet vel utationsed ent nullum vullut ad exeros at. Ismodolor aliquat pratie facil utat niamcortisi esse tie commy nonsequissi.

Lor sim el dolor senit del dui tat alis del ut augue commy nullaorper inim voloreetum nonse vulluptatet esto deliquis alit praessi bla facil irit ulputat verostrud magna con henismodiam et vel del dolor adipis augiamcon henibh exeratuer sisi blam inim zzrillu ptatem quam volore min ute dit wisl ut wiscill aorpero odigna facil il iriusto endreet, consequat ilisi te magna faccum quate dui er sit laoreet vercilit alit velis nonsequat iuscilis amet venissi bla feu feuis do eugait lobor sim.

**Duipsumsan hendip
endre velis nos dolore
dio commy nibh exero
core do elendip el
utpat dolobo.**

WHITE SPACE

↑ *Together with the alignment of the text and images, white space plays an important role in the design of this layout. Clean areas between the images and the text add to the structure of the layout, particularly when the subject matter is also of a structural nature, as with this imagery* *of the Sagrada Família in Barcelona, Spain. These clear areas allow the layout to breathe, and create a sense of calm order in the design. Note the use of dummy Latin text. This is common practice for professional designers if real text is not available when design work begins.*

← *In contrast with the example far left, the white space here creates a very definite frame around the information. The space emphasizes the message and focuses the viewer's attention very effectively on the type. Note that* *the type form is placed slightly above center in the frame. If it were placed dead center, it would appear too low. (This principle also applies when one is framing a picture for hanging on a wall.)*

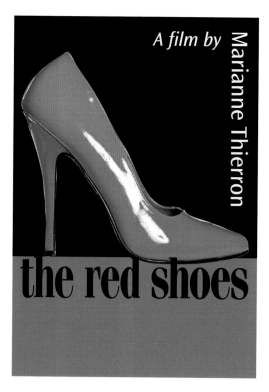

↑ In the first example (from left to right), the negative space above and below the principal form (the shoe) combined with the film title is not helping the layout hold together, and the awkward placement of the credit line is creating some trapped space. In our second example, the use of space has been improved slightly, but the layout is still unsatisfying: the connection between the image of the shoe and the type is lost due to the evident visual separation. However, the red and black panels do help to address this issue to some extent, so it's not completely unsuccessful.

Forms

When you make a layout you'll almost certainly combine several elements, for example, a block of type with an image and a rule. The shapes these combinations produce are known as forms. Think of them as the positive part of the layout, and the space as the negative part. This is a good way to get an understanding of how to manipulate the relationship between form and space to produce a successful layout. Too much positive form makes a layout feel cramped and overdone; too much negative space makes it feel empty and insubstantial. Your decision regarding how to manage this relationship will be governed by what is required of that layout, and the message it needs to convey. For a strong, decisive layout you should utilize very definite contrasts in form and space; for a layout with a quieter feel, a more open relationship between the positive and negative elements is required.

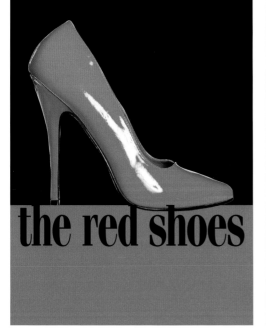

Trapped space

A word of warning—avoid what professional designers call "trapped space." This is basically space enclosed by two or more forms that doesn't do anything to help the structure of the layout. Trapped space is effectively unplanned space as it's not space that you've consciously created. It may be a hole in the middle of a layout between images and text, or an awkward space between juxtaposed forms. Either way, if you notice areas of space that don't appear to serve any purpose, your layout probably needs a rethink.

↑ *Our third example isn't a significant improvement on the first two attempts. Again, it's not entirely unsuccessful, but as a visual it's not particularly exciting either, and the space isn't being used to good effect. However, in our fourth and final example the typography is more dynamic and uses the space under the heel of the shoe to good effect. This, in turn, allows the type to be made bigger, which immediately improves the dynamics of the layout. The main form dominates the space, and the credit line sits neatly beneath without feeling separate from the title. Note that we've used a lighter weight of type for the main headline, enabling us to push the type size up as much as possible. A bolder weight would require more space across the measure and would therefore need to be set smaller to fit the space.*

Grouping

I use an analogy to help design rookies achieve structure in their projects—picture a layout as a flat piece of artwork, and imagine that it's being pulled apart in several directions. If the forms that make up the piece aren't grouped together in a structured way, the design will easily break apart. If, however, the forms all hang together nicely, and if the pulling were to suddenly stop, the layout would spring back together as if it were printed on a sheet of elastic paper. I grant it's a slightly odd analogy, but it works for me.

As someone new to graphic design, your first attempts at a layout may look a little unstructured, but don't be disheartened. It takes time and practice to get the hang of things, and there are one or two tricks to learn that will help you out. A technique professional designers use to create structure in their layouts involves visual grouping, that is, arranging forms to create strong visual relationships. For example, you can surround related forms with a border or panel, connect them using rules, or use different fonts to create clear typographic hierarchies. All these examples work in support of the most obvious way of forming a group, which is simply to place elements close together.

Proximity

A number of forms arranged in close proximity to one another make up a group. No big revelation there! Grouping is very useful for graphic designers because it helps to make complex layouts easier on the eye. For example, you may have a dozen different bits of information making up a poster, but if you arrange that information in two or three groups, the viewer has fewer distinct *areas* of information to decipher. Even simple lists benefit from the application of proximity rules if there are related groups within them.

↓ *The examples below demonstrate three different approaches to grouping and proximity. The first example doesn't rely on grouping—the plane and the two clouds are separate entities within the layout. In the second there are two distinct groups, the clouds and the plane, and I think* *this is probably the most successful layout of the three as it has a nice cohesive quality to it. In the third example, all the components are grouped together in close proximity, which works well enough, but feels a little cramped, and the larger cloud affects readability somewhat.*

However, positioning those elements in close proximity doesn't necessarily create visual harmony. The way the type, images, and graphics interconnect visually always has to be carefully considered or you'll end up with a messy layout. It's a good idea to experiment with a few different arrangements to find out what looks best. Look at the way each form sits against the others, and decide if there are any awkward visual relationships between them. Here's where you need to watch out for that trapped space problem we discussed earlier. You can train yourself to recognize instances where this happens by applying the same kind of logic that you would use if you were arranging furniture in your living room. It's like noticing that two armchairs don't look right pushed together against one wall, so you move one to the other side of the couch to balance up the room.

Spanish Market

Saturday mornings
from 8 until noon in
the Castle Gardens.

The perfect place to
get your fresh food!

Spanish Market

Saturday mornings
from 8 until noon in
the Castle Gardens.

*The perfect place to
get your fresh food!*

Saffron Rice

80g (3oz) unsalted butter
$^1\!/_2$ cinnamon stick
5 whole cardamom pods
3 whole black peppercorns
200g (7oz) basmati rice
1 pinch of saffron threads
sea salt
200g (7oz) Greek yogurt, seasoned with garlic
Crispy caramelized onions

Saffron Rice

80g (3oz) unsalted butter
$^1\!/_2$ cinnamon stick
5 whole cardamom pods
3 whole black peppercorns
200g (7oz) basmati rice
1 pinch of saffron threads
sea salt

*200g (7oz) Greek yogurt, seasoned with garlic
Crispy caramelized onions*

← ↙ *These ingredients lists demonstrate simply how grouping can help to structure information. The upper example makes no distinction between the ingredients of the main dish and the final two entries which are, in fact, the garnish. In the lower example, spaces above the main ingredients and the two garnish items are introduced. This helps separate the components of the dish's ingredients. Further visual grouping is provided by the use of an italic for the garnish, and a bold sans-serif font for the recipe heading.*

↑ *The first example of a flier advertising a Spanish produce market displays little in the way of structure or grouping. The introduction of the colored band containing the "when and where" information in the second example focuses the viewer's attention on the most important text through grouping, and also by emphasis, which we discuss throughout this chapter.*

↓ *These posters advertising Leader's New York concert demonstrate how a combination of grouping, emphasis, and hierarchy can contribute to the success of a design.*

For one night only
at New York City Music Hall
LEADER
plus special guests
September 21 2009
Tickets $18.50
doors 7.30pm open until
late
band on stage at 9.00pm
free drink with prebooked ticket

Appearing at the
New York City Music Hall
6th Avenue, NYC • www.NYcitymusic.com

plus special guests

September 21 2009
Tickets $18.50 • doors 7.30pm • band on stage at 9.00pm

Free drink with a prebooked ticket
Tickets available from the venue box office and online

WRONG!

❶ The typography looks awkward and ugly.

❷ The location and band name are lost amid the rest of the information.

❸ You don't need to say "for one night only" because only one date is shown on the poster.

❹ The information about ticket prices doesn't emphasize the fact that you get a free drink.

❺ The poster doesn't provide any information about how or where to book a ticket.

RIGHT!

❶ The typography is much more effective.

❷ The location and band name are more prominent, and an address and website are listed.

❸ "For one night only" has been dropped from the poster, allowing more space for relevant information.

❹ Ticket information is grouped into a single unit, and that free drink will pull in the crowds.

❺ The all-important information about how to purchase your ticket has been added.

Analyze the way the groups in a layout affect the way your eye travels through the information. Hierarchy and emphasis (*see pages 050–053*) play a large part in this, but proximity is also important. Visually prominent groups will draw your eye from one area of a layout to another, like stepping stones across a stream. Try to ensure that the correct path isn't obscured by extraneous graphic forms that obstruct the flow of information.

Separation

How can separation help to form groups? Well, if you create groups within a layout, and then move those groups further apart to create either emphasis or a clearer hierarchy, you're still maintaining the integrity of each of those groups. Sometimes a layout can really benefit from the introduction of a generous portion of space between the different forms that make up the whole piece. This follows on from our earlier discussion about space and form on pages 042–045.

Cityscape

Images of the city: a new photography exhibition

12th–28th September at the Proud Galleries

↑ *What we have here is a particularly interesting example of separation enhancing the sense of grouping between elements in a layout. The headline title for this photography exhibition is as far away as it can be from the cityscape illustration at the base of the poster. However, the small additional element of illustration above the type helps to group the two separated elements into one cohesive form, adding to the dynamism of the poster's design. Other graphic devices, such as rules and borders (see pages 064–065), can also create structure out of separation.*

Attention!

There are things you can do if you want to draw attention to yourself. You can shout, you can make yourself bigger by standing on a box, or you can wear brightly colored clothing. When creating attention-grabbing graphics, design professionals use techniques that are, in fact, quite similar to things you already know from everyday life.

Size

This may seem kind of obvious when you think about it—make something bigger and it's sure to get noticed. In fact, all will depend on the size of the forms surrounding the item you want to stand out. You won't create much of an effect if, for example, two pieces of type that are meant to contrast with each other are different by only a couple of point sizes. If you want to create real emphasis, make them markedly different in size. The relative sizes of the headings and text here provide an example of this. Remember too that you don't have to make something really big in order to make it distinct from the other forms in the layout. A small image sitting within a large area of empty space will command as much attention as a large image surrounded by lots of other graphic forms.

Position

Feeding straight off this idea of using space to emphasize graphic forms, the positioning of items can have a huge impact on the dynamics within a piece of graphic design. Utilizing both size and position is a great way to make a graphic jump right out at the viewer from a page or website. For example, taking a portion of an image off a page edge so that it crops dynamically, and then enlarging it, can produce a great result. Another way to create emphasis through positioning is to change the angle of an image or piece of typesetting so it contrasts directly with other graphic elements in the piece. Remember that visual excitement will nearly always grab a viewer's attention, so be bold with the positioning of the elements in your layouts to get the maximum effect.

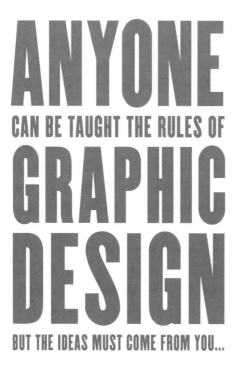

ANYONE
CAN BE TAUGHT THE RULES OF
GRAPHIC
DESIGN
BUT THE IDEAS MUST COME FROM YOU...

↑ *If a particular part of a message needs more emphasis, use the size of the typography to help you. "Anyone" and "graphic design" are the key points here, and the larger point size shouts out the message loud and clear.*

The Pet Store
236 East Street
Open 9.30-5.30

← In this example there
is no noticeable hierarchy,
so the design is pretty
boring. The information
is clear enough, but
nothing draws the eye,
and the message is weak.

**The
Pet Store**
236 East Street • Open 9.30-5.30

← This version of "The
Pet Store" graphic is a big
improvement on the
example shown above.
The image and principal
type dominate and
provide a clear focus in
terms of visual emphasis.
Also, note the pleasing
interaction between
image and type, forming
a basic logo which could
be used separately.

**The
Pet Store**
236 East Street • Open 9.30-5.30

← In this third version the
image of the significantly
enlarged goldfish is also
dynamically cropped to
provide the main visual
emphasis. Note that
angling the image slightly
(forgive the pun) also
increases its attention-
grabbing properties.

Color

The use of color is a great way to create attention-grabbing graphics. Combinations of colors with a significant difference in hue or intensity will create more impact than combinations of colors that are similar in these respects. Hue refers to the color itself, or the shade of a color, and intensity simply refers to a color's strength. Don't be tempted to always go for red when you're choosing an emphasis color (something many nondesigners do) as it can seem a bit of a cliché. Other strong colors are just as punchy when used in the right combination. For the benefit of those affected by red-green color blindness, avoid combining red or orange with a green background. Remember that colors need to work with rather than against the prominent colors appearing in images, so always try to look for harmony as well as contrast between all the elements in your layout. Also, consider whether good old black and white would work best. A graphic in solid black against a white or pale background will really stand out, as will a white graphic reversed out of black or a dark color. Finally, give some thought to how much of the emphasis color you need to use to create the desired effect. An emphasis color used sparingly within a muted color palette can still produce a design full of visual impact.

→ *The colors used in the pattern on the left are strong, but there is little contrast between them so no single color stands out. On the right, the blue and purple harmonize well and have a similar hue, but the yellow is strikingly different and therefore strongly emphasized.*

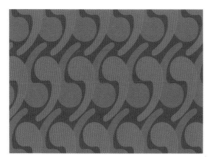

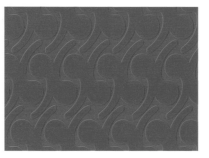

↑ *If you're one of the 7–10% of people who experience red-green color blindness, the pattern above may appear as a single block of color, or as two colors that are very similar.*

↑ *Simple black and white provides the strongest visual contrast you can get, so if a lively color palette isn't what you're after, it's a good choice.*

← ↑ *Designer Chris Rubino has created posters for the Tokion Creativity Now Conferences in New York since 2003. The color choices he makes are key to the standout quality of his designs. The decision to use fonts inspired by woodblock prints and circus posters may not seem appropriate to the cutting-edge nature of the event, but the visual surprise this creates provides a unique quality that sets the posters apart from others on the street.*
www.chrisrubino.com

Surprise!

Building something unexpected into your design will set it apart from the competition and draw attention to it, which is essential under certain circumstances. For example, if you're designing a newspaper advertisement that will appear next to others, take a look at the content of the ads that were run in the previous week's paper. They'll probably be similar from week to week so you'll be able to see what can be done to make yours different and therefore prominent. If they all use a photograph as part of their design, create an illustration for your own ad. The choice of typeface may also help to make your design more engaging. Think about how a font that may not seem appropriate initially could set a design apart, combine it with the right colors or background graphics, and you've got yourself a strikingly different piece of graphic design.

Structure & alignment

Here's where the points we've discussed in the preceding pages begin to come together: space, grouping, hierarchy, and, of course, positioning. All have an important role to play in building the structure of your layout, and good structure leads to effective visual flow.

→ There are three basic alignments from which to choose, the most popular of which is "flush left," also known as "ranged left" or "left-aligned."

Flower arranging classes
Every Sunday at 2:30pm
At the Community Center, Alfriston

→ Alternatively, all the elements of a layout can be moved to a "flush right" position, which could help draw the viewer's eye toward other forms positioned to the right of the piece in a layout.

Flower arranging classes
Every Sunday at 2:30pm
At the Community Center, Alfriston

→ This third option uses a centered arrangement in which all elements align on an axis running through the vertical center of the layout, which draws the eye straight down.

Flower arranging classes
Every Sunday at 2:30pm
At the Community Center, Alfriston

Visual flow

Visual flow is all about directing the viewer through a layout so that they look at the information in the order you want them to. There are simple graphic devices you can use to do this, of course, such as placing arrows to suggest a route through a layout. If you have a series of images that need to be followed, as in a step-by-step series of instructions, you can number them to indicate the sequencing. This kind of directive device makes the ordering obvious to the viewer, but, in addition, the use of space, the positioning of images and text, and the way the forms are grouped will also suggest a direction of visual flow.

Secure the area

One thing that you don't want (unless it's intentional, of course) is a flow that leads the viewer's eye off the edge of a layout. This can be caused by a number of things, but the main culprits are graphics or images with a strong directional element. For example, if you place a left-facing portrait on the left-hand page of a brochure, the viewer's gaze will tend to drift off to the left as well. If the portrait were facing right, toward the center of the layout, the left-to-right flow would be correctly maintained. Use well-proportioned space around a layout's edges to provide a border that will contain the graphics, and group forms in a way that anchors them to the page area you're working with, using positioning and proximity to create visual linkages.

↓ *A disregard for any rules of alignment in the poster on the left results in a very messy layout with no structure. Mixing alignments in this way is never a good idea. Aligning the principal* *typography along the image's edges in the example on the right creates a pleasing form for the main focus of the poster, and the flush-left information at the base is neat and clear.*

VISIT THE BEAUTIFUL ISLAND OF CAPRI

- Tours available Tuesday–Sunday
- Departures 10:00am and 11:30am from Naples port
- Return trip at 7:00pm

- Tickets: 20 euros per person

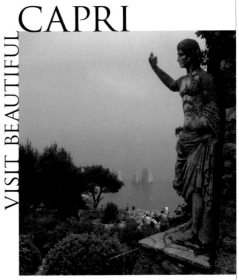

CAPRI

VISIT BEAUTIFUL

- Tours available Tuesday–Sunday
- Departures 10:00am and 11:30am from Naples port
- Return trip at 7:00pm
- Tickets: 20 euros per person

CAPRI

Daily tours:
- 10:00am
- 11:30am
Return trip at 7:00pm

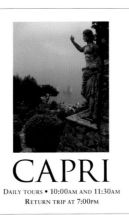

CAPRI

DAILY TOURS • 10:00AM AND 11:30AM
RETURN TRIP AT 7:00PM

← *The flier on the left looks weak because the typography has no defining structure, and the image placement draws the eye away from the information set in the bottom corner. The right-hand example combines centered text with strong emphasis built into the type styling, and this is far more successful.*

→ In this flier for a record fair, the graphic of the turntable is linked neatly with the text through the introduction of a white rule to create visual interactivity. The horizontal division made by the rule also adds dynamism to the layout.

Record Fair

Secondhand CDs & vinyl
Every Sunday morning
8:00am until noon

→ Here, the main type is linked to the secondary text and image through being set over the change in background color. The division is angled to follow the top edge of the turntable in order to create visual harmony, and to add dynamism to the design.

Record Fair

Secondhand CDs & vinyl
Every Sunday morning
8:00am until noon

↑ The white, dotted lines in the examples above represent the imaginary lines your brain draws when registering visual alignment. Learn to take advantage of this when deciding how to align type and images in order to achieve a professional look for your designs.

Bridge the gaps

The interaction between the principal forms that make up your layout will create those linkages. You can achieve them using simple devices, such as small overlaps of text and image, or by introducing tinted panels or decorative images to fill visual gaps. It's a bit like imagining that you could walk through your layout without having to touch the ground (or paper). I'm not saying that every single element of the design has to be linked in some way, but if you use visual links of this kind within the main forms of your layout, everything should hang together nicely. And don't forget to keep an eye out for trapped space.

Visual connections

To further enhance the sense of structure between different forms in a layout, pay close attention to alignments. The idea here is never to position individual elements or forms randomly, but to place them in a way which visually connects them with other forms. The interesting thing about using alignment is that you aren't adding any physical elements to the layout; the aligned forms are connected *virtually* by the lines that your brain draws for you. Alignment also helps you to make decisions about the positioning of elements and forms. For example, it will dictate where you should place a logo and address details on a design for stationery, or where an image that relates to a particular block of text should be positioned.

Alignment is arguably the most important of all the techniques that help to create visual harmony. For this reason, it's important to observe the rules of alignment as closely as you can. There aren't many instances I can think of in which they won't help to make your design work look more professional.

Grids are good

For a graphics newcomer, designing a grid on which to position the elements in a layout may seem a bit over-the-top. You may be thinking, "Why not simply place the images and text where they look right?" For simple, one-off layouts this works perfectly well, but if you're planning to design something more ambitious, such as a brochure or newsletter, you really should think about designing a grid first. Professional graphic designers love grids, and rightly so!

What is a grid?

In graphic design terms, a grid separates a page into vertical and horizontal divisions. These divisions could include:

* margins at the edges of the page;
* columns dividing the page vertically;
* rows dividing the page horizontally;
* spaces between blocks of type and/or images; and
* spaces between individual rows of type, also known as the *baseline grid*.

A grid provides you with a modular system on which to build a layout methodically. To demonstrate how this works, the grid used for the layout of this book is drawn on these pages. From this you can see how a grid will help you to make decisions about where to position items across multiple pages. Grids encourage consistency, which is important for projects with more than a few pages, and will also speed up the layout process.

← *These spreads, taken from earlier in this chapter, demonstrate further how the various forms that make up the layout sit on the underlying structure of the grid. Not everything has to line up, of course. Note that the text in this caption aligns with the bottom of the grid's area, but not to each baseline in the same way that the running text does. This is because the smaller caption text requires less space between each line. Captions need to align with the image they relate to, but not necessarily to the rest of the running text in a layout.*

Choosing measurements

If you were of a mind to read about the more complex aspects of grid design you would find that there are many geometrical theories concerning how best to proportion a grid. However, I'm going to keep it simple and say that there are no set rules about the size of margins, or about the spacing or number of columns and rows. Those decisions are yours to make. I usually begin by settling on a rough measurement for the margins at the top and sides of a page, and decide what the bottom margin should be after a bit of visual experimentation. A good way to do this is to draw a box filled with a colored tint (if you are using a computer), or to cut out an oblong of colored paper (if you are working manually) to roughly represent the *text area* of the page. Text area is the term commonly used by graphic designers to describe the total area enclosed by all four margins on a page. You can then move the box/paper around on the page until it feels right visually, then measure the outer margins. It's a purely visual thing—everyone has a different opinion as to what looks right. All other horizontal and vertical measurements can be built around this basic frame.

↖ ↑ Grids are built from simple frames, like the example on the far left. The text area can then be divided into multiple columns, and subdivided horizontally into rows to create a cellular grid.

↗ → This spread from the RotoVision book Character Design for Graphic Novels illustrates how a grid with multiple horizontal and vertical divisions (cells) can provide maximum flexibility for the placement of images and text on a page. Here, the complete spread is broken down into 16 vertical and 16 horizontal divisions. (Illustrations by Brendan Cahill. www.brendancahill.com)

Drawing the grid

If you're using a computer, the grid will be represented by nonprinting guidelines that the software generates, behind the images and text, based on the measurements you enter in the relevant dialog boxes. If you're not, there are a couple of options. The first is to draw up your grid on a sheet of tracing or layout paper which you can lay over your artwork to check positioning and alignments. The second, a little more practical, is to draw a very faint grid on the actual paper or board which can be erased once your artwork is complete. If you're planning to photocopy the artwork once it's completed, use a light-blue pencil to rule up the grid and you won't need to remove the lines at all. Photocopiers don't pick up the blue lines, and only the elements of the artwork that need to reproduce will show up on the copies.

Breaking the grid

Rules are made to be broken, and the same thing goes for page grids. If you want to introduce one or two visual surprises into your design, break out of the grid occasionally by extending images or forms into the margins, or even completely off the page edges. You could also place elements at an angle to create another level of visual dynamism, but be careful not to overdo it or the layout will look messy and undesigned. Unexpected elements will add texture and pace to a design, and this will encourage the viewer to keep turning the pages.

↓ → All the sample grids shown on this spread are built around a common text area, but the way the area is divided varies. Immediately below we have a basic three-column grid, and below that a four-column grid with an area at top left reserved for the main heading. Note that the four-column grid allows the images to be sized with a little more flexibility. To the right, our original three-column grid is further divided to give a four-deep cellular grid, which is great for laying out smaller images in a "tiled" arrangement. Below that is a grid with a narrower outside column into which text can extend. The final example uses both the four- and the three-column grid. As you can see, using grids need not restrict your layout options.

Japanese Style

Margins

When deciding on the measurements for a grid, try making the top margin slightly smaller than the bottom margin so the text area doesn't look as though it's sliding down the page. Also, if you're working with facing pages (that is, spreads, as in an open magazine or book), make the inner margins smaller than the outer margins for a more even distribution of material across the spread. Because the inner margins meet in the center (or gutter) of the spread they effectively double up, and the combined margin will look too wide compared with the outer margins if you don't compensate for this.

Japanese Style

Japanese Style

The
Ingredients
of Graphic
Design

3

Rules & borders

Wherever they appear in a layout, the principal function of rules and borders is clear. They frame, support, divide, point at, and emphasize the text and imagery that make up the content of the piece.

Plain rules and borders are generally used in a purely functional capacity, often to delineate the edges of images, for annotation (labeling illustrations), or for the division of areas within a layout. This means they're often secondary to the main content, but don't underestimate the importance of this supporting role. Rules and borders can also become styling elements that contribute to the feeling you want to create for your design work.

0.25pt
0.5pt
1pt
2pt
4pt
8pt
Double line
Double line with varied weights
Triple line
Dotted line
Dashed line
Diamond line
Wavy line
Directional end
Bar start and end
Circle end
Arrow start and end

Rules

A rule is a straight line which may be solid, dotted, dashed, or decorative, depending on what is appropriate for the specific design. You can also add an *endcap* to a rule, which could be a dot, a bar, an arrowhead, a circle, or whatever works for you. The thickness, or *weight*, of a rule is normally, but not strictly, specified in points rather than inches or millimeters. One point is approximately $1/64$in or 0.35mm. When deciding to use a stylized rule as part of a design, think about whether or not it's really necessary, as it's easy to go over-the-top when you're starting out. Rules should underpin text and images; they should not have a greater visual prominence than other, more important elements of the layout.

If you're not using a computer to produce your artwork, you can purchase special technical pens which produce very accurate rules of a specific weight. Rotring is an excellent brand, with both refillable and disposable models in its range.

↑ *The thickness of a rule is normally specified in points, some examples of which are shown above. Stylized rules, or rules with endcaps, are available as built-in options in your chosen layout application, but if you're feeling brave, try creating your own rule styles for projects.*

Borders

As with rules, borders should generally support the material they are surrounding without overwhelming it. The exception to this would be borders that are an integral part of an image—in such a case elaborate styling may well be entirely appropriate. Borders are great for defining key areas of a layout, or for emphasizing important bits of information, and the styling can make a huge difference to the way a layout is perceived. When choosing a direction for border styling, pay close attention to what happens on the corners as these are the areas of a border that draw the eye most.

↑ The thickness of a border, like a rule, is specified in points. The style of a border should never overwhelm the material contained within it: borders should be considered very much supporting elements in any layout. Details at the corners of borders will always draw the eye, so exercise caution when using elaborate corner styling.

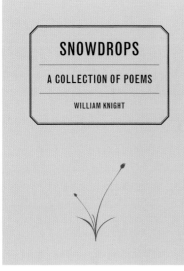

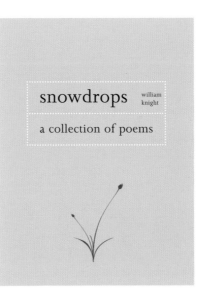

← These examples show how a border can affect the way a piece of work is perceived. The cover on the far left suggests that the book is a collection of traditional poetry because of the classic styling of the borders; the second styling gives the impression that the content is much more contemporary.

Photograph or illustration?

A single image is capable of saying as much, or perhaps more, than paragraphs of words. All you have to do is look at a beautiful image of a tropical beach and you immediately feel the need to go on vacation.

The emotional response that imagery provokes is key to many graphic design projects that need to convey a strong message, and the choice of photography or illustration to produce your images will play a major role in generating the feel of your design.

Making a choice

It's likely that many of you own a camera, probably a digital model, and making your own photographic (rather than illustrated) images for a project may seem the easiest option. In practical terms, a lack of confidence in your own drawing skills may also persuade you to opt for this choice. (Incidentally, don't feel down if drawing isn't your strong point—many professional graphic designers, myself included, are not skilled illustrators.) However, the fact that you must first find the scene you need before you can photograph it does complicate this approach: finding that scene is not always possible. You can always turn to an alternative source such as an image library, but it's more fulfilling if you try to create your own images.

Model Steam Train

Suitable for children of 3 years and up

Model Steam Train

Suitable for children of 3 years and up

no.12

←⬉ These two examples are conveying the same basic message about a tourist attraction, but they feel very different from one another. The photographic imagery is much more "grown-up" and may attract the attention of older rail enthusiasts, whereas the illustrated version says "kids' steam train," and would appeal to a much younger audience. The appropriateness of each option depends very much on what the advertiser wishes to achieve.

But there is more to image choice than simple practicalities. The selection of photography or illustration isn't just about the ease with which you can produce your imagery, it's also about how the final piece will look, and about the message it must convey. A colorful illustration can add a real sense of fun or character to a piece of design, particularly when, for example, the piece is aimed at children. Also, illustration can be used to convey a message in a more abstract way than photography, through simple colors and shapes. It is very important to bear in mind that an illustration doesn't have to be an accurate rendering of an object or scene. It can be anything you want it to be, and in that sense the illustration option can sometimes be more adventurous, and more creatively satisfying.

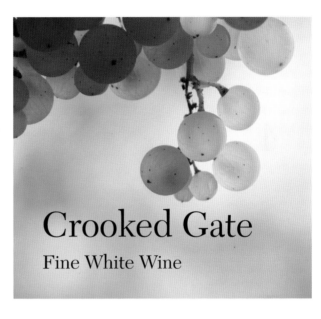

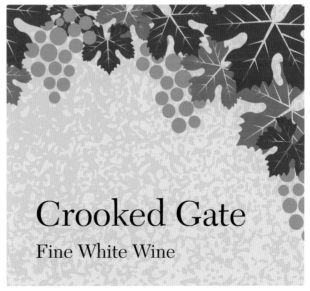

Using digital images

When working with a computer your images will, of course, be in a digital format, and there are a few important considerations to take on board if you want to achieve the best quality when you print your projects on an inkjet or laser printer. This gets a little bit technical, but don't be put off as a little knowledge goes a long way when it comes to working with digital files.

Image resolution

Digital images are made up of millions of tiny squares called pixels, and the more pixels there are *per inch* of image, the better the image quality will be. High-end digital cameras with a large megapixel rating (*see* page 036) record lots of pixels per inch (ppi), so images can be used at large sizes without a loss of quality. Ideally an image should be around 300ppi when placed in a layout in order to produce a good print. If you have access to software such as Adobe Photoshop or Photoshop Elements you can open up an image on your computer to check the original resolution, but if you don't, it's not a major problem—your camera's manual will include this information.

Most digital cameras allow you to set various resolutions for shooting, so check that your camera is set to the best-quality option when taking pictures for your projects. Now for the technical bit—the relationship between resolution and image size. I have a camera that records images at 72ppi (rather than the ideal 300ppi), but the image size

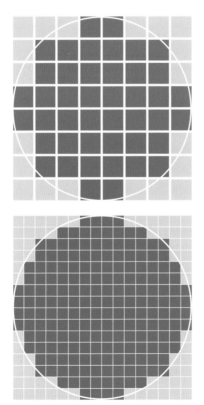

← The diagrams to the left represent halftone dots. A printed image is made up of a matrix of equally spaced dots of varying size to produce color and tone. You can see them if you look through a magnifying glass. The top diagram shows a halftone dot of 8 × 8 pixels, the lower is 16 × 16 pixels. The more pixels that appear in each halftone dot, the better quality the output will be.

→ The Image Size palette in Photoshop and Photoshop Elements (pictured here) allows you to resize your digital images from 72ppi up to 300ppi. The image in question started out in-camera as a 72ppi image measuring 685.8 × 914.75mm (27 x 36in).

is large, at 3,456 × 2,304 pixels, or 48 × 32in (120 × 80cm). If the image is placed in a layout, then reduced to a smaller size from the original, the resolution goes up because the pixels are concentrated into a smaller space.

Reducing an image of this size and resolution to a width of 11½in (30cm) will increase the print resolution to the 300ppi ideal. On the flip side, if you enlarge an image beyond its original size, the resolution goes down and the quality is degraded. As an experiment, enlarge an image on your computer screen by 300–400% and you'll notice that you start to see the actual pixels appearing in the picture as it gets larger. This is called *pixellation*.

To sum this up, watch for pixellation when you print your work out. If you can see pixels appearing in your images, you're using them at too low a resolution and should either reduce their size in your layout, or try to create or obtain a replacement image at a higher original resolution.

Learn more about: Image Size

OK
Cancel
Help

Pixel Dimensions: 14.4M
Width: 1944   pixels
Height: 2592   pixels

Document Size:
Width: 16.46   cm
Height: 21.95   cm
Resolution: 300   pixels/inch

Scale Styles
Constrain Proportions
Resample Image: Bicubic

↑ The images shown above are of different resolutions. The upper image is 300ppi, and the lower image 72ppi. We chose this image specifically because the fine details in the roof structure demonstrate how pixellation can occur at lower resolutions.

Images in layouts

It's difficult to offer advice about how to use images in your layouts as this depends on many different factors which change between projects. Instead, here are a few questions to ask yourself when thinking about your design.

* How large (or small) should your images be used, based on their importance to the message of the layout?

* How should the images interact with other elements of the layout, such as type, bringing into play techniques discussed in Chapter two?

* Do you need to crop into the image to show a detail, remove a distracting visual element from an image's edge, or simply to improve the composition?

* Do you need to add a border to the image to define its edges?

* Could you change the image's border to a round or freehand shape to add dynamism to your layout, or even cut out an image from its background?

If you consider these basic points at the beginning of a project, it will help you make some important decisions early on, making the design work much easier overall. And remember, you can always change your mind as nothing is ever set in stone.

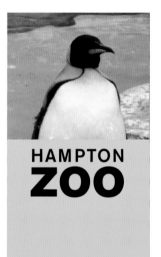

↑ ↗ These examples demonstrate just how many simple layout combinations you can achieve with one image and a short typographic statement. Colored panels, cutout images, and cropping are all tools frequently used by professional designers.

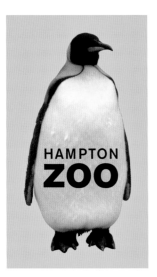

HAMPTON
ZOO

Personal image libraries

You never know when you might happen across a photo opportunity for a future design project. If you have a compact camera that fits into your bag or pocket, get into the habit of carrying it with you all the time so that you can collect visual material to build into your own personal image library. Digital cameras are ideal for this because you don't have to worry about the cost. You can snap anything that looks interesting and edit the material later (everything from portraits and landscapes to abstract backgrounds are potentially useful), and the regular practice will improve your photographic skills.

Photography © Tony Seddon

Color theory

It wouldn't be an exaggeration to say that color is the most influential tool at a designer's disposal when it comes to transmitting a message through a piece of graphic design. Color provides a very powerful means of creating mood and tone, and understanding the relationships that exist between colors will help you to realize your creative thoughts more readily.

The color wheel

Before we get into any discussions about which colors work well together, it's worth talking about color wheels. These work by placing three primary colors at three equidistant points around a circle. You can build color wheels by starting out with red, green, and blue, which are the three colors used by TV and computer screens. You can also use the standard process printing colors: magenta, cyan, and yellow. However, we'll stick with the traditional artists' wheel, which is based on red, yellow, and blue.

If you divide the spaces by mixing adjacent colors, the colors that appear at each halfway point are known as the secondary colors. Whether you are working on a computer, which produces new colors electronically, or physically mixing paint, the principle is the same. In our example, working counter-clockwise, these will be orange (red mixed with yellow), green (yellow mixed with blue), and violet (blue mixed with red). If you then divide those spaces even further you get the tertiary colors, which are red-orange and yellow-orange, yellow-green and blue-green, and blue-violet and red-violet. Dividing these spaces many more times eventually produces a smooth gradation which moves through the entire visible spectrum of colors.

The diagram here shows how the secondary and tertiary colors are achieved through interaction with one another. Color wheels are great tools for working out good color combinations.

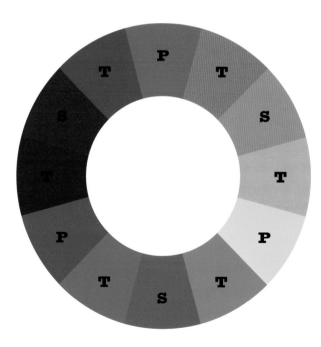

⬆ A color wheel that uses red, yellow, and blue as its primary (P) colors. The secondary (S) colors opposite each primary are green, violet, and orange. Mixing the primaries with their adjacent secondary colors creates the tertiary (T) colors (clockwise from red): red-orange and yellow-orange; yellow-green and blue-green; blue-violet and red-violet.

Additive & subtractive mixing

I won't get too technical here as this section is really about how to choose colors, but it's worth explaining briefly how these two types of mixing work. Additive mixing is what happens on your computer screen, where red, green, and blue light combine to form the different colors. Subtractive mixing is what happens when inks or pigments are printed to produce different colors, where light reflected back from the paper's surface creates the different colors we see. You'll find that printed images often look different from your computer's display; given the difference between the way the colors are created, it's not surprising that this happens.

↑ *The professional color-specification systems used by practicing designers are very expensive; as an alternative, use a free paint-swatch chart from* *your local hardware store when you need to devise new color schemes for your projects. Just remember that you'll have to work out what* *the correct CMYK (see page 076) color values are by visual matching if you want to print the color accurately on your inkjet or laser printer.*

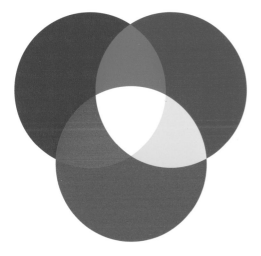 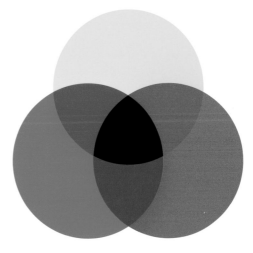

↑ ↗ *The additive mix (left) involves red, green, and blue light mixing to form white, with yellow, magenta, and cyan light forming as secondary* *colors. This is how color is created on a computer screen. The subtractive mix (right) involves cyan, magenta, and yellow pigments absorbing* *light to reflect different colors—all three together form black. This is how we see printed colors.*

Choosing color

So—how do you set about choosing which colors to use in combination for your latest design project? It's entirely subjective, of course—it's up to you what message you want to convey—but you can use a color wheel to help with your choices.

Using the color wheel

There are several ways of working with the color wheel, each of which will provide you with markedly different combinations. The first is to take colors that appear at equidistant points around the wheel. This will provide you with a set of distinct colors, and you can choose as many as you need, but for this example, let's say you need four colors for your illustration. Pick a strong color for areas of the illustration that define edges and borders, and use colors of lesser prominence to fill the areas in between.

The second method is to pick four colors that are adjacent to each other on the wheel. This will provide a harmonious range of colors that won't necessarily provide a strong signature color, but will nevertheless provide a good range of hues that work well together.

The third method is to choose colors that are directly opposite each other on the wheel. Obviously this only works for pairs of colors, so try picking two colors that you then combine with simple black and white, or a pair that will work with any other two-color choices.

→ *These combinations were created using the color-wheel methods discussed on these pages. You can choose as large a range of colors as you wish using these methods, depending on how many divisions the wheel you are using has. Take a look at the website http://kuler.adobe.com/ which is run by Adobe. It features hundreds of color combinations submitted by contributors, and is one of my most visited bookmarks.*

Equidistant points

Adjacent points

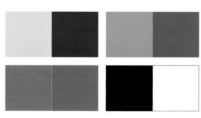

Complementary color sets

Monochromatic color

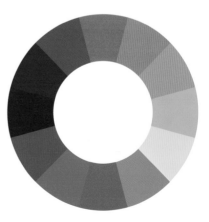

Don't forget that you can always start with just one color, then use different shades to create a monochromatic color palette for your piece. If you do this it's best to start with a color near one of the three primary colors in order to give you the freedom to create a decent range of lighter tints. If you start with a light color, the available range will be limited.

I like this method for choosing colors as it doesn't rely on the use of a computer. You can use it working with paint, using colored markers or pencils, or even cut paper for collages. In fact, I would recommend that you get your hands dirty and use some paint rather than just stick to the computer as it will help you develop a real-world sense of the *quantities* of color that go into the final mix.

➜ ⬇ To demonstrate how different color schemes work for an actual illustration, we've created a few examples for you. As an exercise, try to match the color combinations to the method we used to pick them. The color wheel from page 072 is repeated for easy reference.

Color harmony

Color harmony isn't simply about whether or not colors work together; it's also about the mood you want your design to create. If you want a calm feeling for the piece, go for complementary colors, but if you want something bolder, a clashing combination might be just the ticket.

Personal color libraries

If I come across a great combination of colors when I'm working on a project, I add them to a document I keep handy on my computer. I do this by drawing a series of boxes side by side and filling them with the colors following the order in which I think they work best. In addition, for easy reference, I note down the combination of CMYK percentages (*see* box, below left) that make up the colors. If you go one step further and arrange them by mood or theme, you'll eventually build up an invaluable color-reference library. I've included a few of my favorites here, organized by theme, to help you get your own library started.

CMYK

CMYK is an abbreviation for cyan, magenta, yellow, and black. K is used to represent black as it is referred to by printers as the "key" color. In full-color printing, all colors are achieved through a combination of tints of cyan, magenta, yellow, and black inks, otherwise known as the process colors. Take a close look (with a magnifying glass if you have one) at a color photograph in a magazine and you'll be able to see the dots that make up the image in the four different colors. A light color is achieved with small dots which reveal more of the paper beneath the ink; increasingly large dots make up darker colors. Solid areas of color are created from 100% tints which cover the paper entirely. Refer to the manual you received with your software to find out how you can create CMYK colors for your own layouts.

How to interpret the color charts

- 020/030/040/000
- 020/060/040/000
- 060/070/080/000
- 030/030/030/070

Each example combines four CMYK colors to build a range of hues that reflect a mood or style you may want to create for a project. The colors are specified as percentages of cyan, magenta, yellow, and black: for example, 20% cyan, 30% magenta, 40% yellow, and 0% black is 020/030/040/000.

Refreshing

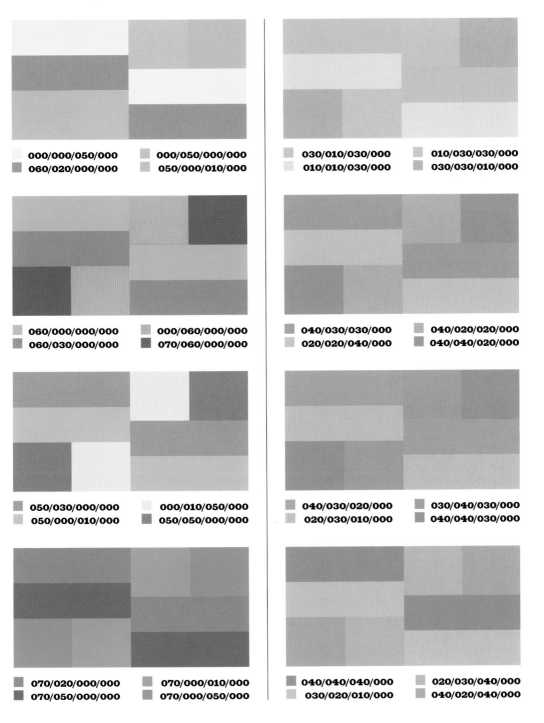

000/000/050/000
060/020/000/000

000/050/000/000
050/000/010/000

060/000/000/000
060/030/000/000

000/060/000/000
070/060/000/000

050/030/000/000
050/000/010/000

000/010/050/000
050/050/000/000

070/020/000/000
070/050/000/000

070/000/010/000
070/000/050/000

Natural & tranquil

030/010/030/000
010/010/030/000

010/030/030/000
030/030/010/000

040/030/030/000
020/020/040/000

040/020/020/000
040/040/020/000

040/030/020/000
020/030/010/000

030/040/030/000
040/040/030/000

040/040/040/000
030/020/010/000

020/030/040/000
040/020/040/000

Organic & fruity

Tropical & lush

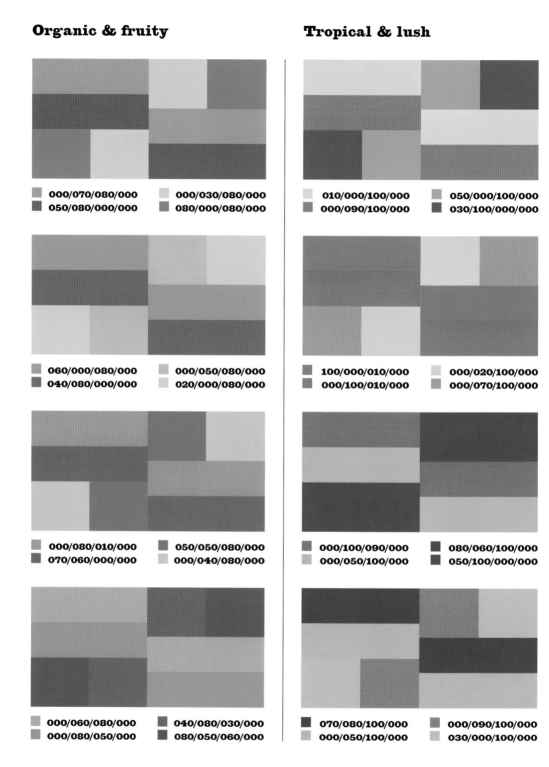

000/070/080/000
050/080/000/000

000/030/080/000
080/000/080/000

010/000/100/000
000/090/100/000

050/000/100/000
030/100/000/000

060/000/080/000
040/080/000/000

000/050/080/000
020/000/080/000

100/000/010/000
000/100/010/000

000/020/100/000
000/070/100/000

000/080/010/000
070/060/000/000

050/050/080/000
000/040/080/000

000/100/090/000
000/050/100/000

080/060/100/000
050/100/000/000

000/060/080/000
000/080/050/000

040/080/030/000
080/050/060/000

070/080/100/000
000/050/100/000

000/090/100/000
030/000/100/000

Ethnic & cultural

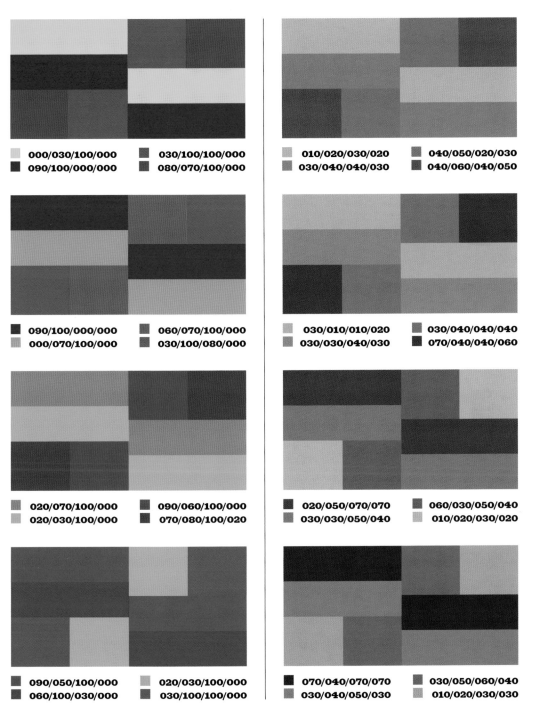

■ 000/030/100/000   ■ 030/100/100/000
■ 090/100/000/000   ■ 080/070/100/000

■ 090/100/000/000   ■ 060/070/100/000
■ 000/070/100/000   ■ 030/100/080/000

■ 020/070/100/000   ■ 090/060/100/000
■ 020/030/100/000   ■ 070/080/100/020

■ 090/050/100/000   ■ 020/030/100/000
■ 060/100/030/000   ■ 030/100/100/000

Quiet & subdued

■ 010/020/030/020   ■ 040/050/020/030
■ 030/040/040/030   ■ 040/060/040/050

■ 030/010/010/020   ■ 030/040/040/040
■ 030/030/040/030   ■ 070/040/040/060

■ 020/050/070/070   ■ 060/030/050/040
■ 030/030/050/040   ■ 010/020/030/020

■ 070/040/070/070   ■ 030/050/060/040
■ 030/040/050/030   ■ 010/020/030/030

Cool & watery

Hot & humid

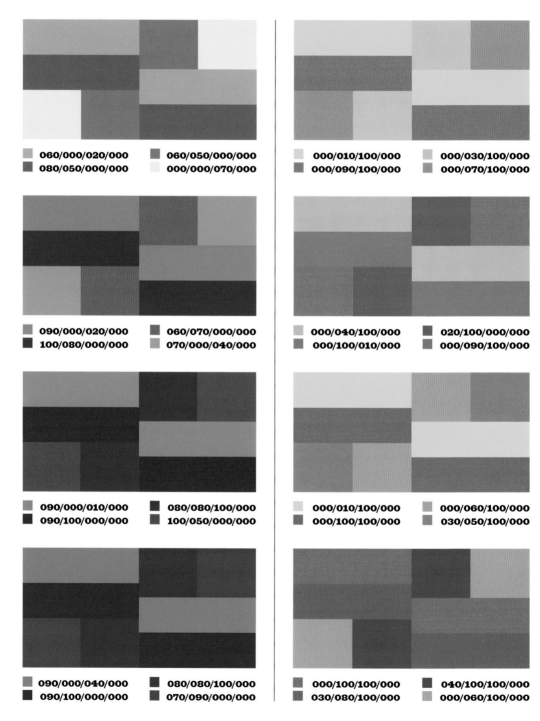

060/000/020/000   060/050/000/000
080/050/000/000   000/000/070/000

000/010/100/000   000/030/100/000
000/090/100/000   000/070/100/000

090/000/020/000   060/070/000/000
100/080/000/000   070/000/040/000

000/040/100/000   020/100/000/000
000/100/010/000   000/090/100/000

090/000/010/000   080/080/100/000
090/100/000/000   100/050/000/000

000/010/100/000   000/060/100/000
000/100/100/000   030/050/100/000

090/000/040/000   080/080/100/000
090/100/000/000   070/090/000/000

000/100/100/000   040/100/100/000
030/080/100/000   000/060/100/000

Elegant

Stylishly chic

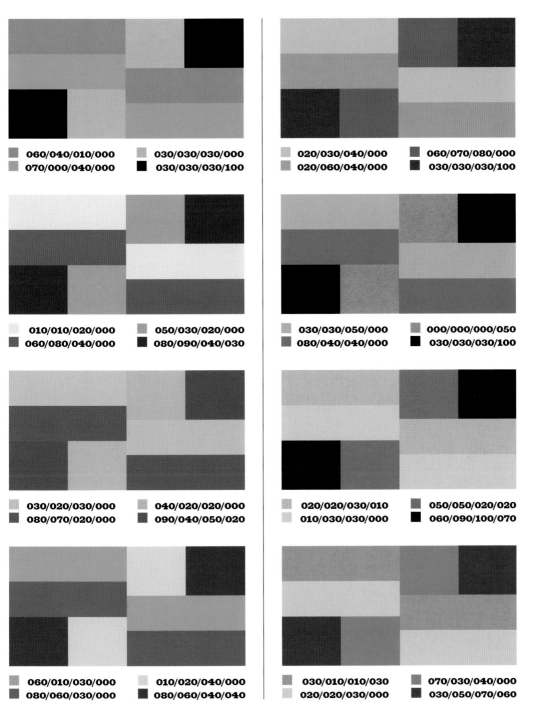

Elegant

060/040/010/000
070/000/040/000
030/030/030/000
030/030/030/100

010/010/020/000
060/080/040/000
050/030/020/000
080/090/040/030

030/020/030/000
080/070/020/000
040/020/020/000
090/040/050/020

060/010/030/000
080/060/030/000
010/020/040/000
080/060/040/040

Stylishly chic

020/030/040/000
020/060/040/000
060/070/080/000
030/030/030/100

030/030/050/000
080/040/040/000
000/000/000/050
030/030/030/100

020/020/030/010
010/030/030/000
050/050/020/020
060/090/100/070

030/010/010/030
020/020/030/000
070/030/040/000
030/050/070/060

Type

Where do I start? Type is something about which I and most other professional graphic designers are completely obsessive. I realize this may sound odd to nondesigners, but it really is true. A beautifully designed typeface is probably the purest form of graphic design there is, and good type and typography form the bedrock of pretty much all graphic design projects.

While we talk about type, I'm going to assume you're using a computer to produce your projects. It's perfectly acceptable (and sometimes appropriate) to draw type by hand, but if you want to produce professional-looking typography, you'll need to work with a PC or Mac.

Fonts

Let's begin by covering the basics of type categorization, as you'll encounter these terms when you look at typefaces in any detail. First of all, a collection of type characters is known as a font. The average font contains all the standard letters and numbers, plus all punctuation, and various special accent and other characters. Collections of fonts that

Abcde

Serif font

Abcde

Sans-serif font

↑ *The fundamental difference between serif and sans-serif fonts is what happens at the end of the strokes. Serif fonts have small horizontal and vertical details added to the ends of the major* strokes; sans-serif fonts do not. The term "sans" is derived from the French for "without," i.e. without serifs. Our sample fonts are Caslon (serif) and Univers 55 (sans serif).

↓ *The three categories of serif font are illustrated below. Old-style serifs have a rounded, classical look; modern serifs are flat and angular; and slab serifs are usually more chunky, combining squared edges and curves. These fonts are, from left to right, Caslon 224, Didot, and Clarendon.*

→ *There are a number of typographic terms you may come across when reading about fonts. The most common are illustrated at right. (The font used is Univers 55.)*

Old-style serif

Modern serif

Slab serif

represent various versions of the same font design (*italic* or *oblique*, **bold**, and so on) are referred to as type families.

There are several ways to categorize fonts, the most common groupings being *serif* and *sans serif*. Serif fonts are those that have small, pointed details added to the ends of the character's strokes, and sans-serif fonts are (you guessed it) those that don't. Other common categories are *script*, *display*, *novelty*, and *dingbat* or *symbol*. Each type of font has its place in terms of usage, and it's not so difficult to work out which kind is appropriate for whatever application you may choose. For example, you probably wouldn't choose a novelty font for an invitation to a particularly serious event, but you might well use one if you were designing a party invitation or birthday card.

ABCDEFGHIJKLMNOPQRSTUVWXYZ
abcdefghijklmnopqrstuvwxyz 0123456789

ABCDEFGHIJKLMNOPQRSTUVWXYZ
abcdefghijklmnopqrstuvwxyz 0123456789

ABCDEFGHIJKLMNOPQRSTUVWXYZ
abcdefghijklmnopqrstuvwxyz 0123456789

ABCDEFGHIJKLMNOPQRSTUVWXYZ
abcdefghijklmnopqrstuvwxyz 0123456789

ABCDEFGHIJKLMNOPQRSTUVWXYZ
abcdefghijklmnopqrstuvwxyz 0123456789

ABCDEFGHIJKLMNOPQRSTUVWXYZ
abcdefghijklmnopqrstuvwxyz 0123456789

ABCDEFGHIJKLMNOPQRSTUVWXYZ
abcdefghijklmnopqrstuvwxyz 0123456789

ABCDEFGHIJKLMNOPQRSTUVWXYZ
abcdefghijklmnopqrstuvwxyz 0123456789

ABCDEFGHIJKLMNOPQRSTUVWXYZ
abcdefghijklmnopqrstuvwxyz 0123456789

ABCDEFGHIJKLMNOPQRSTUVWXYZ
abcdefghijklmnopqrstuvwxyz 0123456789

ABCDEFGHIJKLMNOPQRSTUVWXYZ
abcdefghijklmnopqrstuvwxyz 012345

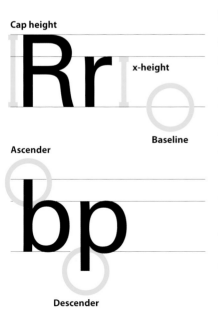

Cap height

x-height

Baseline

Ascender

Descender

↑ *Some font families carry a particularly extensive range of weights. The example here is a selection from the Akzidenz Grotesk family. From top to bottom we have: Akzidenz Grotesk Regular, Italic, Medium, Medium Italic, Bold, Bold Italic, Condensed, Bold Condensed, Extra Bold Condensed, Extended, and finally, Bold Extended.*

Choosing a font

I mentioned on the previous spread that type is the main ingredient for most graphic design projects. The whole feel of a project will be governed by the font you choose. Luckily there are loads to choose from, and lots of online vendors selling good-quality fonts for a relatively small outlay.

Centaur
Bembo
Bodoni
Garamond
Meridien
Sabon

The downside is that the more fonts there are to choose from, the harder the choice becomes. For professional designers, visiting font websites is like being in a supermarket-sized candy store. However, the reality is that the vast majority of available fonts are not very well designed, so beware of cheap imitations. The trick is to build up a list of favorites. This can be as extensive as you like, but I would advise keeping it to a manageable size so that it is easy to browse through. Our list of favorites might help you get started with your own.

Each font category has a few basic characteristics you should be aware of: this will help you choose fonts that look appropriate and professional in your finished projects.

Serif fonts

Serif fonts are identified by the small, pointed details, or serifs, at the ends of their strokes. Serif fonts have a certain air of authority about them which makes them a good choice for more serious applications. They are also generally easier to read over long periods of time, or when there is a large amount of text in a single block. The serifs help to guide the reader's eye along the horizontal lines of text, and the character shapes are often more distinct from one another at smaller sizes. This is why serif fonts are used extensively in the design of novels and newspapers.

Sans-serif fonts

It is reasonable to suggest that sans-serif fonts look a little more modern and a little less formal than serif fonts. This is a bit of a generalization, but in principle the observation holds true. Sans-serif fonts are great for things like big punchy headlines, or for tables and charts. They're also good for typesetting text that runs over relatively short widths, but can be more difficult for the eye to follow over long line lengths than serif fonts. We chose a sans-serif font (Myriad Pro) for the running text in this book for these reasons.

← → This is just a small selection of the enormous range of fonts available to purchase today. The fact that you can now browse the sites of dozens of online font retailers, and preview fonts before you buy them, makes it easy to find suitable fonts for your project, but it also makes the final decision harder because there are so many to choose from. The fonts on the left are serif, and on the right, sans serif.

Dax Condensed
Eurostile
Futura
Helvetica 45
Interstate
MetaBook
Rockwell
Univers

Blackoak

Armada Bold

FoundryGridnik

Caslon Open Face

Frankfurter

Mason Bold

Linoscript

Künstler Script

Marker

Radio AM

Snell Roundhand

Display fonts

If you need to make a big statement in a headline or on a poster, a display font may be the best choice. They are often fairly stylized, and, as a result, are not always well suited for use with running text. Display font type families are usually limited to only one or two weights.

Script fonts

There is a close relationship between script fonts and traditional hand-rendered calligraphy. Script fonts are particularly useful for elegant headlines or ornamental display, but they're pretty hopeless for running text as the complex nature of the characters makes readability difficult at small point sizes. Avoid using script fonts in a clichéd way—a trap design novices often fall into. A well-designed italic serif is often a better choice than an overly fussy script.

←→ The number of display, script, and symbol fonts available is considerable. Novelty fonts are as numerous again, and can be easily sourced, but beware of quality issues—many are not well designed, and do little to suggest a sense of professionalism.

Novelty fonts

The sky is the limit with novelty fonts. There are thousands of fonts of this type, ranging from the genuinely well designed and useful to the ridiculously awful. The use of a badly designed novelty font is the easiest way to flag your design work as "nonprofessional." Some novelty fonts look great, but be careful with your choices and always question whether or not a good-quality, well-designed serif or sans-serif font would serve you better.

Dingbat or symbol fonts

These fonts are composed of a series of graphic symbols assigned to each letter of the standard alphabet. They're useful for things like bullet-point lists or for diagrams where the main font doesn't have a wide variety of distinctive symbols within its own character set. Specialist dingbat fonts containing symbols that can be applied to signage, or maps and charts, are also particularly useful.

The fonts on the left, from Blackoak to Mason Bold, are display; and from Linoscript to Snell Roundhand, script. Those on the right, from Bleeding Cowboys to Rosewood, are novelty; and the remainder are dingbat or symbol fonts.

ABCDEFGHI
JKLMNOPQR
STUVWXYZ
abcdefghi
jklmnopqr
stuvwxyz
1234567890
!.?,&$

Hand-rendering fonts

I mentioned at the beginning of this section that I'm assuming you'll use a computer (PC or Mac) to produce your design projects. However, if you don't own any layout software, such as Adobe InDesign or QuarkXPress, you can always hand-render your type. In fact, hand-rendering type is sometimes a more appropriate option, particularly if you want a "crafted" feel for your project. Furthermore, hand-rendering type helps you to learn why different fonts are designed and drawn the way they are: it is an excellent way to improve your letterspacing skills (*see* page 093). It's not a practical option for running text, of course, but for headlines, or for posters with only a small amount of typographic content, it is perfectly feasible.

First of all you'll need to find a sample of the typeface you want to use. There are many books on the market full of sample fonts which you can either trace or photocopy. Dover Books (*see* page 218 for listing) is a good place to look for books of this kind. Alternatively, if you do have a PC, you can type out a full alphabet of your chosen typeface at the size you require, including upper- and lowercase characters, numerals, and any basic punctuation or symbols you may need. You can use any word-processing package to do this. Practice makes perfect, so take a couple of test runs with your chosen typeface before you attempt to produce any finished artwork.

handmade
graphics
handmade graphics
handmade graphics
handmade
graphics
handmade graphics
handmade
graphics

↖ ← *This sample type sheet (of a font named Viva) contains all the basic characters you may need to hand-render a headline. Try a few alternative typefaces if you aren't sure* *which you'd like to use in your final design, and take care to observe the rules of legibility and readability that we discuss in the next few spreads of this book.*

Some of our favorite fonts

Serif
Baskerville
Bembo
Bodoni
Caslon
Garamond
Perpetua
Sabon
Walbaum

Sans serif
Avant Garde
DIN
Frutiger
Futura
Gill Sans
Helvetica Neue
Interstate
Univers

Script
Kuenstler Script
Linoscript
Metro Script
Shelley Allegro
Snell Roundhand

Display
Armada
Caslon Open Face
Impact
Mason
FRANKFURTER

Novelty
BLACKCURRANT
Bleeding Cowboys
Dot Matrix
LCD
ROSEWOOD

Dingbat

Carta

European Pi

FF Dingbats

Woodtype Ornaments

Zapf Dingbats

NB: all samples are shown at 18pt

Legibility & readability

Choosing which font to use on the basis of style and feel is only half the story, as legibility and readability are also of paramount importance. Remember, it's not about whether or not you can discern and read the type personally, but whether the people the piece is aimed at can.

Different people will have differing requirements when it comes to reading the text laid out as part of your graphic design project. Readers with poor eyesight will need some help with legibility, and very young children who are learning to read won't be able to recognize complicated letterforms. Because of this, you must always carefully consider the target audience for the piece, and select your fonts accordingly.

Font legibility

FONT LEGIBILITY

F O N T L E G I B I L I T Y

FONT LEGIBILITY

Font legibility

Font legibility

FONT LEGIBILITY

Font suitability

Serif fonts are generally considered the easiest to read when you're dealing with a lot of type. Sans-serif fonts also provide a high degree of legibility, but script and novelty fonts may present a challenge, depending on the complexity of the font's design. Also, fonts that have very narrow character shapes (ultra-condensed fonts), or very wide characters (extended fonts) are not always the best choice for running text, and their use should, on the whole, be restricted to larger headlines and labels.

← *This selection of type demonstrates how the degree of legibility can vary from one font to another. The serif font at the top is highly legible, as is the sans-serif font below it. Adding space between characters can improve legibility in some cases, but should be used with caution for anything other than sans-serif fonts. The script font is virtually unreadable. The condensed and expanded examples below that are acceptably legible, but only because there are just a couple of words displayed. The novelty font is fun (and indeed readable), but really not suitable for anything other than headlines and titles.*

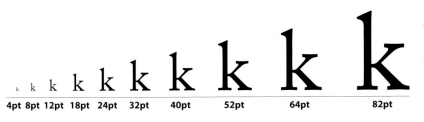

k k k k k k k k k k
4pt 8pt 12pt 18pt 24pt 32pt 40pt 52pt 64pt 82pt

← Font size is expressed in points, with a point (pt) being 0.353mm (0.014in). The text in this book is set in 8pt Myriad Pro Light; 8pt is a popular choice for running text.

Regarding legibility and readability, there are several key factors to take into account as well as that of font choice. These are:

* the size at which you use the font;
* whether it is upper- (capital) or lowercase;
* the color applied to the type;
* the color behind the type;
* how the type is spaced between individual characters (kerning) and words (tracking); and
* how the type is spaced between individual lines (leading).

→ This sample is set in, from top to bottom, Minion Pro regular, italic, and bold; Didot Regular; Glypha 55 Roman; and Benton Gothic Regular. All are suitable choices for running text, depending on the feel you wish to achieve with your design. Look at the qualities of these paragraphs. Each has a different level of readability. Note also that the line breaks differ from one paragraph to the next because of the space each font fills. The first paragraph, set in a serif font, is the winner in terms of readability and space efficiency. The extra detail of the serif italic makes the text slightly harder to read; it is best not to use italics to set large amounts of text.

Rat ad eugait, veleseq uamet, sed delit la faccumm odipit ing euguero dit, qui bla am veliquamet nit nullan velit augiam, sit dolor in ulla accumsan ut vel.

Rat ad eugait, veleseq uamet, sed delit la faccumm odipit ing euguero dit, qui bla am veliquamet nit nullan velit augiam, sit dolores in ulla accumsan ut vel.

Rat ad eugait, veleseq uamet, sed delit la faccumm odipit ing euguero dit, qui bla am veliquamet nit nullan velit augiam, sit dolor in ulla accumsan ut vel.

Rat ad eugait, veleseq uamet, sed delit la faccumm odipit ing euguero dit, qui bla am veliquamet nit nullan velit augiam, sit dolor in ulla.

Rat ad eugait, veleseq uamet, sed delit la faccum odipit ing euguero dit, qui bla am veliqua met nit null ans velit augiam, sit dolores.

Rat ad eugait, veleseq uamet, sed delit la faccum odipit ing euguero dit, qui bla am veliquamet nit nullan velitas augiam, sit dolor ulla.

RAT AD EUGAIT, VELESQ UAMET, SED DELIT LA FACCUMM ODIPIT ING EUGUER DIT QUI BLA.

Rat ad eugait, veleseq uamet, sed delit la faccumm odipit ing euguero dit, qui bla am veliqua nit nullan velit augiam.

Rat ad eugait, veleseq uamet, sed delit la faccum odipit ing euguero dit, qui bla am veliquamet nit nullan velit sit luptat.

← *Setting running text in ALL CAPS (in this case News Gothic Roman) is rarely a good idea. Text set in caps tends to give the impression that the author is shouting, and readability can be reduced. Script-style fonts are also less suitable for running text due to readability issues, so exercise caution, and choose a script font only if (a) the amount of text is minimal; and (b) the subject matter lends itself wholeheartedly to that particular style choice (e.g. a comic-book layout).*

Rat ad eugait, veleseq amet sedir delit la faccum odipit euguero dit, quier bla am veliqua met nit nullan velit augiam, dolores in ulla accum sa ut vel ing ergo iliquam, velesto corem velo ustet dolore venis.

Rat ad eugait, veleseq amet sedir delit la faccum odipit euguero dit, quier bla am veliqua met nit nullan velit augiam, dolores in ulla accum sa ut vel ing ergo iliquam, velesto corem velo ustet dolore venis.

Rat ad eugait, veleseq amet sedir delit la faccum odipit euguero dit, quier bla am veliqua met nit nullan velit augiam, dolores in ulla accum sa ut vel ing ergo iliquam, velesto corem velo ustet dolore venis.

Rat ad eugait, veleseq amet sedir delit la faccum odipit euguero dit, quier bla am veliqua met nit nullan velit augiam, dolor in ulla accum sa ut vel ing ergo iliquam, velesto corem velo ustet dolore venis.

Rat ad eugait, veleseq amet sedir delit la faccum odipit euguero dit, quier bla am veliqua met nit nullan velit augiam, dolor in ulla accum sa ut vel ing ergo iliquam, velesto corem velo ustet.

← *Leading, the space between the individual lines of type, affects the ease with which the eye can pick up the start of each new line of text. The 12pt type in this example is shown with 12pt, 15pt, and 20pt leading, respectively. The 15pt is the most successful for this font.*

↑ *Intercharacter spacing affects the personality and readability of type considerably. Very tight spacing, as in the top example, restricts the ease with which individual words can be scanned, and widely spaced characters can make individual words run into one another.*

Size

There isn't a simple set of rules to apply to font size and legibility, and using a large font size isn't necessarily going to make it easier to read. The size at which you can use a font will always, at least to an extent, be dictated by the nature of the design you're working on. The correct approach is first to pick a font that you think will work well in terms of readability and style, then decide how large (or small) the font has to be in relation to the available space in the layout. For example, if you have a series of headings at the top of every page of a brochure, find which is the longest and base your choices for size and font on that heading. This will maximize the legibility and ensure that all the other headings will fit.

Case

In general, if you have a block of running text to integrate into a layout, it'll work best in upper- and lowercase. It's not necessarily wrong to set a block of text using all capitals (all-caps), but my advice is to restrict the use of all-caps to headings, short blocks of text, or captions. An additional problem with lots of uppercase setting is that it can have the effect of making it feel as though the author is shouting at you.

Color

We talked about using color to grab attention on page 052, and similar rules apply here. Typographic legibility is best achieved through the use of color combinations with a significant difference in hue or intensity, with black and white as the strongest contrast of all. Don't forget red-green color blindness, which affects 7–10% of men (though only 0.4% of women).

Spacing & leading

Intercharacter spacing (kerning) and overall spacing between characters and words (tracking) play a significant role. It depends on the font being used, but adding space between characters can sometimes improve readability. However, don't overdo it. If the spaces between characters start to become as wide as the spaces between words, the words will appear to run into one another and readability will be lost. To a lesser extent, the space between lines of text (leading) is a factor too. If your chosen font has a large x-height (the height of the font's lowercase x), the leading should be wider than that given to a font with a smaller x-height. Like type sizes, leading is specified in points, and a good rule of thumb when determining the amount of leading to apply is to add 2–4 points to the size of the type. This text is set in Myriad Pro Light, 8pt, and the leading is 11.5pt.

→ *Type set using highly contrasting colors is generally the most successful. Black on white, or white out of black, work better than any other combination. Colors of a very similar hue should be combined only where the design requires subtlety.*

Rat ad eugait, veleseq uamet, sed delit la faccum odipit ing euguero dit, qui bla amos veliqua met nit nullan velit augiam, sit dolor ulla accuma.

Rat ad eugait, veleseq uamet, sed delit la faccum odipit ing euguero dit, qui bla amos veliqua met nit nullan velit augiam, sit dolor ulla accuma.

Alignment

This section follows on directly from the discussion about legibility and readability. Text alignment plays a large part in determining the ease with which type can be read. However, there are other important factors that come into play when deciding which option to go with.

Rat ad eugait, veleseq uamet, sed deli la coma velesto faccumm odipit in euguero dit, qui bla am veliquamet nit nullan velit augiam, sit dolores in ulla accumsan ergo ut vel.

Rat ad eugait, veleseq uamet, sed deli la coma velesto faccumm odipit in euguero dit, qui bla am veliquamet nit nullan velit augiam, sit dolores in ulla accumsan ergo ut vel.

Rat ad eugait, veleseq uamet, sed deli la coma velesto faccumm odipit in euguero dit, qui bla am veliquamet nit nullan velit augiam, sit dolores in ulla accumsan ergo ut vel.

Rat ad eugait, veleseq uamet, sed deli la coma velesto faccumm odipit in euguero dit, qui bla am veliquamet nit nullan velit augiam, sit dolores in ulla accumsan ergo ut vel.

The basics

There are four kinds of alignment commonly used by graphic designers: ranged left, ranged right, justified, and centered. Ranged left (or flush left) refers to text that aligns at the beginning of each line, but has a ragged edge on the right side of the column, formed by wherever the last word on each line finishes. Ranged right is the reverse of this, with the alignment moved to the right side and the ragged edge to the left, at the start of each line of text. Justified is the term used to describe text that uses small variations in the letter and word spacing to ensure that the text aligns down both sides of a column. Centered text aligns down the center of the text block with a ragged edge running down both sides.

There are practical as well as aesthetic reasons for choosing one type of alignment over another. Readability is, of course, a factor. Some designers would argue that justified alignment is best for lots of running text, as in a novel, because it is easier for the eye to scan back for the beginning of the next line. Personally, I'm not sure this argument stands up, as the amount of leading (*see* pages 092–093) applied also plays a part in this, and in my opinion ranged-left text works just as well in this regard. I tend to choose whether or not to range left or justify text for aesthetic reasons initially, and then consider other, more practical factors, such as how the text is breaking at the end of each line, after a bit of experimentation.

← *Examples, from top to bottom, of flush left, flush right, justified, and centered text.*

Ranged-right text has its uses, but it's not an option that's used much for running text as it's harder for readers to scan from line to line. However, it can look good as part of a layout where you have a short run of text to the left of an image or other graphic element.

Centered text also has its uses and can look great when used properly, but be careful not to mix centered with ranged-left or justified text in such a way that awkward visual associations are created. For example, it wouldn't work if you centered a headline above ranged-left text, as the spacing before and after the headline wouldn't be equal in relation to the line of text below.

Take care when setting a headline

Take care when setting a headline

↑ *When setting large type in a headline, balance up the line lengths as best you can. How you achieve this will* *obviously depend on the wording of the headline. The top example, with the overly long first line, feels unbalanced; the change* *in the line break in the second setting makes it more pleasing visually.*

Rat ad eugait, veleseq uamet, sed delit la faccum odipit ing euguer dit, qui bla am veliqua met nit null ans velit augiam, sit dolor.

Essequam conse dunt wis num zzrit nisl dipsustin ea faccum nit autpate min henit at, velis situ molorem alis alit ut incipsu sciull num.

← *Avoid isolated single words at the ends of paragraphs. These are referred to as "widows" in typesetting terminology. The term "widow" also describes the final line of a paragraph isolated at the top of the following page or column.*

Headline
Rat ad eugait, velese uam faccum odipit in euguer dit, qui bla amis veliqua met nit null ans velista augiam, sit dolor raessim.

Rat ad eugait, veleseq uamet, sed delit la faccum odipit ing euguer dit, qui bla am veliqua met nit null ans velit augiam, sit dolor.

Essequam conse dunt wis num zzrit nisl dipsustin ea faccum nit autpate min henit at, velis situ molorem alis alit ut incipsu sciull uptat dolor vel enim num.

← *Paragraphs that follow on from one another in running text should be "indented" to indicate clearly that a new paragraph has begun. The depth of the indent is a purely visual decision, and will vary depending on the layout and the font being used.*

Headline
Rat ad eugait, velese uam faccum odipit in euguer dit, qui bla amis veliqua met nit null ans velista augiam, sit dolor raessim.

↑ *A centered headline mixed with flush-left text looks awkward; mixing centered and justified alignments is more successful.*

Considering column widths

The column width, also commonly referred to as the measure, is the width of any given block of text. This book is designed around a five-column grid, with a measure of 24.5mm (just under 1in), and a gap of 4mm ($^5/_{32}$in) between each column. This means the text you're currently reading, which is set over two columns, has a measure of 53mm (24.5 + 4 + 24.5). Combining this measure with the 8pt Myriad Pro Light allows us to fit roughly 6–9 words on each line, meaning the ratio of column width to word count is working acceptably well with our choice of ranged-left alignment. To find a rough word-per-line count, type a couple of paragraphs and work out the average number of words per line. Remember that too many words per line can affect readability adversely; as a very general rule of thumb, 60–70 characters per line is a good average. However, if we were to reduce the column width for whatever reason we would run into problems with the number of words we could fit on any one line, particularly if any words were especially long. When the text is ranged left, long words over short column measures create ugly line breaks with overly large gaps at the ends of lines. Switching to justified alignment is unlikely to improve matters under these circumstances, as this would create ugly gaps between words in the middle of the column, so it's important to ensure that you settle on a suitable column width at the beginning of a design project.

Hyphenation

If you can't avoid using a narrow measure in your layout, you can always introduce hyphenation to help deal with awkward line breaks. You can split a word over two lines by adding a hyphen between syllables in longer words. Take care not to be too free with your use of hyphenation though. You should avoid adding hyphens at the ends of adjacent lines, for example, and only hyphenate between syllables that have at least three characters in them, or the word will become difficult to read. You can hyphenate ranged-left text if you wish, but I tend to add hyphens only to justified text.

Rat ad eugait, veleseq uamet, sed deli coma velesto faccum odipit in eug dit, qui bla am veliquamet nit nullantira velit augiam, si dolor ullat accum-sanco ergonat vel. Im etum iusci exer atie vel diam. Ex elitsuscip et la feuisis cidui-simzrit augueri liquip euipit aliquat, commy nis

← *The flush-left text shown here has been hyphenated. There are no strict typographic rules against this, and it looks OK, but I tend not to hyphenate flush-left text. I believe it is better to edit the text if line breaks are visually awkward.*

Rat ad eugait, veleseq uamet, sed deli coma velesto faccum odipit in eug dit, qui bla am veliquamet nit nullantira velit augiam, si dolor ullat accum-sanco ergonat vel. Im etumi usci exer atie vel diam. Exelit-suscip et la feuisis ciduisimzrit augueri liquip euipit aliquat, commy nis

← *Hyphenating justified text is, in my view, more acceptable, and it helps to avoid bad spacing between words set over short measures. Don't use too many hyphens, turn off auto-hyphenation if it is the default setting in your software, and don't allow hyphens to appear on successive lines.*

Rat ad eugait, veleseq uamet, sed deli la coma velesto faccum odipit in euguero dit, qui bla am veliquamet nit nullantira velit augiam, sit dolores in ulla accumsan ergo ut vel. Im etum iusci exer atie vel diam zzriusc ipsummy nulput nissississi. Ip exeros aut vulluptat. Tie vel ing et nulla faci ting ea feui tem dolore magnim dolorperit diamet essen euissecte facinim ing et iure feugiam, coreet, sum delenim vel ut prat vel ullutat iuscil dolore dunt volor si tem nonum. Giat iliquismod min eros nonulla putpat. Ut aut irillaore tem volessim.

Rat ad eugait, veleseq uamet, sed deli la coma velesto faccum odipit in euguero dit, qui bla am veliquamet nit nullantira velit augiam, sit dolores in ulla accum san ergo ut vel. Im etum iusci exer atie vel diam zzriusc ipsum nulput nissississi. Ip exeros aut

vulluptat. Tie vel ing et nulla faci ting ea feui tem dolore magnim dolorperit diamet essen euiss ecte facinim ing et iure feugiam, coreet, sum delenim vel ut prat vel ullutat iuscil dolore dunt volor si tem nonum. Rat sent do od magnis.

↑ ← *Long measures are very difficult to scan, and it's easy to accidentally reread or skip successive lines. It is better to split a long measure into two separate columns in order to alleviate the problem.*

Rat ad eugait, veleseq uamet, sed deli coma velesto faccum odipit in eug dit, qui bla am veliquamet nit nullantira velit augiam, si dolor ullat accumsanco ergonat vel. Im etum iusci exer atie vel diam.

Rat ad eugait, veleseq uamet, sed deli coma velesto faccum odipit in eug dit, qui bla am veliquamet nit nullantira velit augiam, si dolor ullat accumsanco ergonat vel. Im etum iusci exer atie vel diam.

← *Flush-left text doesn't suffer from uneven word spacing as font settings equalize the spacing throughout a paragraph. However, it can be a real problem with justified text, especially over short measures, as shown in the example here.*

Rat ad eugait, velesq uamet, sed deli la coma velesto faccum odipit in euguero dit, qui bla am veliqua met nit nullantira velit augiam, sit in dolor in ulla accum san ergo ut vel. Im

etum iusci exer atie vel diam zzriusc ipsum nulput nissi sissi. Ip exeros aut vulluptat. Tie vel ing et nulla faci ting ea feui tem dolore et magnim dolorperit diamet essen euiss

ecte facinim ing et iure feugiam, coreet, sum delenim vel ut prat vel ullutat iuscil dolore dunt volor si tem nonum. Rat sent do od magnis.

← *If you have to use a short measure, choose a condensed font for your layout. This will enable you to fit more words on each line, and thus avoid ugly line breaks and bad word spacing. Remember though, ultra-condensed fonts can be hard to read.*

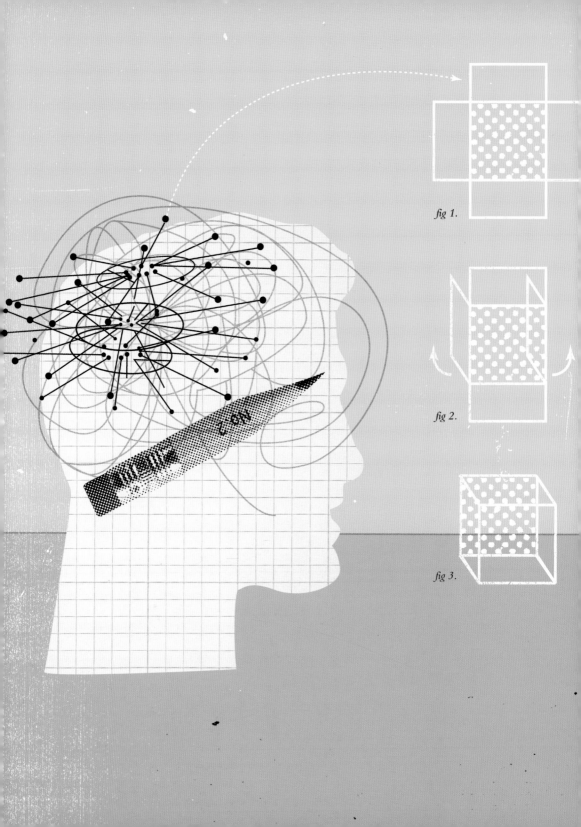

fig 1.

fig 2.

fig 3.

4

Making It

Preparing images

Here's the scenario. You've been out and about taking some shots for your latest design project with your digital camera, but when you download them to your computer they look variously too dark, too red, too fuzzy, and so on. These are all problems that can be fixed quite easily with image-editing software.

If you're not particularly computer literate and haven't used image-editing software before, don't worry; many common problems don't require much knowledge or training to fix. Adobe Photoshop Elements (www.adobe.com; see page 024) is inexpensive and very easy to use. It's a powerful application considering its price, and I'll use it here to demonstrate some basic image-correction techniques. If you own and use a different application, these basic techniques are still relevant as most applications use similar terminology and tools.

Color correction

All digital cameras, even expensive SLRs, sometimes capture images with a slight color cast. Images might look a little too red or blue, depending on the lighting conditions when the photographs were taken. This can be balanced out very easily using the color adjustment features in Photoshop Elements. If you're completely new to this kind of software there's a neat feature that guides you through the color correction process with step-by-step instructions on-screen. Once your confidence grows try out the other options, such as the *Color Variations* palette which allows you to click on preview windows to see the end result before you commit to the adjustment. Everything is highly automated and intuitive.

↖ ← *If you are new to image editing, you can correct images easily with Adobe Photoshop Elements by using the automated features listed to the right of the main application window. However, autocorrection doesn't always give the best results, so it is worth* *getting to grips with the interactive editing features by experimenting with an image that needs some adjustment. The screen shot to the left shows how to access the Color Variations palette via the Enhance menu.*

Before

After

Color relationships

It is useful to remember which additive and subtractive colors lie opposite each other in the color wheel (*see* pages 072–073). The arrows on the wheel below indicate that removing red from an image increases the level of cyan, removing green increases magenta, and removing blue increases yellow. The preview images in the Photoshop Elements Color Variations palette show this color relationship clearly.

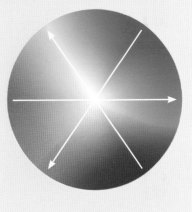

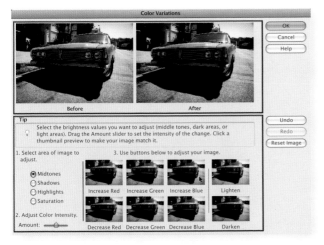

← *The Color Variations palette features Before and After windows so you can always see the cumulative effect your adjustments are having on the original image. By clicking on the small images at the bottom of the palette you can increase or decrease the amount of red, green, or blue in the original, and adjust its lightness or darkness. Check buttons to the left of the palette designate which areas of the image will be affected by your adjustments, and a slider controls the amount of color intensity you will apply with each adjustment. Experiment with this, or with any of the other adjustment palettes, and you will soon be editing images with confidence.*

⬇ ➡ The amazing Shadows/Highlights adjustment feature will help you rescue images with areas of extreme contrast which would otherwise be impossible to adjust without a lot of complex retouching.

Before

After

Shadows & highlights

For fixing images with lots of overly dark shadows and too-bright highlights, the killer feature, which I think is little short of miraculous, is the *Shadow/Highlight* adjustment, accessed via the *Enhance > Adjust Lighting* menu. The palette contains sliders that allow you to lighten shadows and darken highlights independently of one another, and in addition you can adjust midtone contrast to balance things up when you're happy with the other settings.

Experiment with this tool on an image you would otherwise find difficult to print successfully, and you'll be amazed at how much detail can be brought out, particularly in the shadows. The settings you need to use will vary from image to image, so trial and error is the name of the game here.

Sharpening

All images taken with a digital camera tend to be slightly soft, even with spot-on focusing. If an image you've taken is excessively blurred due to camera shake or because the subject was fast-moving, there's not a great deal you can do to save it. However, if the blurring is slight, you may be able to sharpen the image up enough to improve the reproduction quality. Photoshop Elements provides you with several sharpening options, but I think *Unsharp Mask*, accessed via the *Enhance > Adjust Color* menu, is the best choice. The method I always follow is to start with a high Amount value of 200–250% (depending on how blurred your original is), a low Radius value of 1, and a Threshold setting of 0. This will most likely look oversharpened and unnatural, with a white halo effect appearing along edges within the image. If you then increase the Threshold value slowly, your picture will gradually smooth out. Once you've reached a point at which the image looks right, click OK and you're done.

Before

After

Unsharp Mask

OK

Cancel

☑ Preview

100%

Amount: 200 %

Radius: 1.0 pixels

Threshold: 12 levels

← *For most images, an Amount setting of 200%, a Radius setting of 1 pixel, and a Threshold setting of 0 is a pretty good place to start. With these settings applied, the image will probably look too sharp and therefore unnatural, but a gradual increase of the Threshold value will slowly smooth the image out until it looks just right.*

DIY printing

Most of you will have some kind of printer at home next to your computer, but how do you get the best from it when printing your graphic design projects? There are a few basic pointers that will help you to achieve quality when outputting your work.

↑ *Printers like the Epson Stylus Photo 1400 are perfect for graphics and photography enthusiasts,* *and can output on paper up to A3+ (B+) in size.* *Courtesy of Epson.*

Choosing the right printer

There are so many printers to choose from these days, it can be confusing. It's best to check out current reviews and pricing when choosing a new model, but I will say that for all-round use you can't beat an inkjet. The color output will generally be better than that from a laser printer, and despite today's low prices, an inkjet is still cheaper than a laser printer. A machine capable of printing on paper up to A4 or letter size (210 × 297mm/$8^1/_8$ × $11^5/_8$in) may be enough for your needs, but an A3+ or Super B model (330 × 483mm/13 × 19in) will be much better if you want to print larger posters, for example.

Paper & ink

I can't stress enough how important it is to use good-quality paper that's intended for use in inkjets to achieve top-quality output, particularly if there's a lot of color coverage. If you use cheap photocopy paper for anything other than black-and-white text output, the results will never look great. If you're printing basic layouts, use a better-quality paper that has a coated surface which will hold the ink. Check the manufacturer's recommendations for use, printed on the packaging, before you buy. Inkjets use liquid ink that's wet when applied, so highly absorbent paper won't do. If you're printing photographs, go for a specialist photo paper—matte or glossy depending on your taste—and see how much better the results can be.

In terms of ink choice, cartridges manufactured by top brands such as Canon and Epson are much better than the low-cost "compatible" brands, and will be more accurate for color image output. If you only need to print text or nonphotographic color it's not so important, but if you need good image output quality, you won't achieve it with cheaper products.

↑ *The Canon PIXMA iP4500 is a high-quality inkjet capable of printing fine detail and smooth color gradients at high resolution, either from a computer or directly from your digital camera.*

It uses a five-color ink system that includes a dye-based black to add depth and contrast to your printed output. Courtesy of Canon.

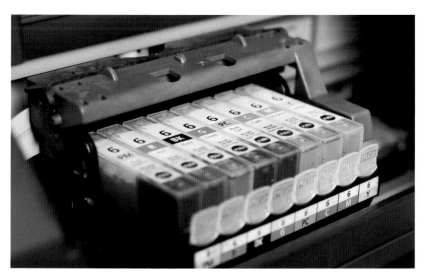

← *Many inkjets use single-ink systems. These are much more economical than systems which use cartridges that combine colors, as you never have to discard unused ink. Printers with the highest specifications introduce colors beyond the standard cyan, magenta, yellow, and black in order to print colors that would other-wise be difficult to replicate. The printer here also has pale magenta, red, green, and pale cyan cartridges.*

Preparing artwork

If your design project can't be printed using your own inkjet or laser printer, you'll have to source a professional printer to get the job done. As nondesigners you're likely to be approaching the subject of artwork preparation with no knowledge whatsoever. A daunting prospect in some ways, but there's a simple solution to this—talk to your printer.

Any printer worth their salt will be more than willing to advise you on any and all aspects of how you prepare your artwork. It's in their interest to do this as well-prepared artwork means less work for them when getting the material ready for printing. Requirements will vary from one printer to another and the way you prepare your material will depend on the service offered by the printer you choose to work with. Many printing companies are now turning to digital output as a standard service option because of the competitive cost, and the speed with which jobs can be printed and delivered. This is good news for design beginners with small budgets and a restricted knowledge of print production.

First steps

This may sound a bit obvious, but many people new to artwork preparation don't think about the first vital step in the process—the final check. If you've been working on a project for a while, it's easy to miss lots of little details that will let the job down and reduce its potential to appear as professional-quality design. Consistency is a major factor, especially if your project involves lots of type with various levels of headings and so on.

Here are a few things to look out for:

* incorrect spellings and missing punctuation;
* consistency of font choice and type sizes across the whole layout;
* consistency of spacing between images, text, rules, and borders;
* consistency of border and rule weights;
* bad crops which cut awkwardly through important areas of images;
* bad alignments or groupings, and awkward or trapped space;
* color combinations that work against each other visually; and
* consistency of positioning for elements of the design that repeat on different pages throughout the layout.

→ When you feel that your project is ready to go to the printers, we recommend that you print the whole project out just one last time. Checking a layout on paper often draws your eye to errors that you might miss if you were checking it on-screen. It's also a good idea to send a printout of your project to the printer along with the artwork so that they have some kind of visual reference to follow.

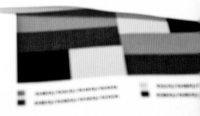

The FINEPRINT Co.

Please ensure that the following specifications are followed when supplying artwork for repro and print.

• All artwork must include at least 3mm (⅛in) of bleed on all edges to allow for trimming.

• All images and text must be at least 8mm (⅜in) within the trim edges as trimming accuracy can only be guaranteed as accurate to within 1.5mm (¹⁄₁₆in).

• Ensure that any unused images on printable areas of the artwork have been removed from the files you supply.

• Please include a printed proof with all supplied artwork, particularly if the printed items are to be folded.

• All images must be placed at a suitable resolution (ideally 300dpi) to guarantee high-quality results. The Fineprint Co. cannot accept responsibility for low-quality print that is supplied at an unsuitable resolution.

• Unless specified, all printing is considered as full color, and work must be supplied as CMYK. Please specify any spot colors or special finishes you require in a separate markup.

• All fonts must be embedded or converted to outlines.

↑ *Most printers will have a list of their ideal requirements for artwork preparation; make sure you discuss any specific issues with them before you send an artwork.*

Talking print

Regardless of whether or not you've used a computer to produce your artwork, your printer will be able to tell you exactly how you should deliver it. If you're in a position to choose a printer early on in a project, go and speak to them before you start putting your artwork together as you may save yourself a lot of hassle further down the line. I would advise that for the first few projects you tackle, don't try to run before you can walk; let the printer deal with the prepress issues, even it means paying a little more to get the job done. You'll soon begin to pick up the tricks (and jargon) of the trade, and, as a result, you'll be able to take on more of the artwork preparation yourself.

And that's it!

Now that we've covered the techniques you need to design and realize your own ideas, it's time to get started. The next chapter features 20 pieces of work which we think represent a typical range of graphic design projects you may wish to tackle yourselves.

Get a proof

Whatever you do, don't allow a job to be printed before you've seen a proof which has been produced and supplied by the printers themselves. If you don't insist on this and the job isn't printed correctly, you have very little recourse. A proof that has been seen and approved by you is known as a "contract proof" and it is just that—a contract between you and the printer which states that the printer must match what you have seen and signed off. Your printer will be able to explain the various types of proof they can provide for you.

↓ *Any comments you make with regard to errors or changes to a color proof must be clearly marked and returned to the printer.*

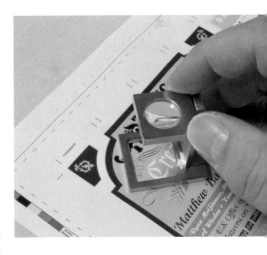

↑ *Checking color proofs is part of a professional designer's role for any project they're involved in. Color proofs are often referred to as "contract proofs," as a printer is obliged to match the final printed output to the color proof you have checked and signed off.*

INCREASE
CONTRAST
ACROSS
IMAGE.

ADD 10% YELLOW
TO BACKGROUND
PATTERN.

REMOVE
BLUE CAST

5

The
Projects

Memos

Memos are generally pretty workaday affairs. If you're the recipient of a memo it normally means that you'll have something else to add to your to-do list, and if it looks boring it's far more likely you'll set it aside, and possibly forget it. Memos don't have to look dull, but they must be clear and easy to read. Be wary of overdoing the styling, or your memo may not be taken seriously.

1 The key points

The most important bits of information, aside from the content of the memo itself, are who it's from, who it's to, what it's about, and when it was sent out. Make sure that you list these pieces of information clearly as a header at the top of the page.

Memora

TO:

FROM:

SUBJECT:

DATE:

1

Operations Department

2

2 Brand it

If you're sending the memo out from a specific department, make sure it's clearly indicated somewhere on the memo's layout. Somewhere near the bottom works well as it constitutes a kind of signature when placed in that area.

Memorandum

3

3 Add some character

Memos don't have to be straight black-and-white. Why not add a little color to the rules or borders, giving a visual lift to the design without going over-the-top? Many of you will have access to color inkjets or lasers, so this is very easy and inexpensive to achieve.

→ *The finished design for our memo has taken the styling just a little further by using an attractive and approachable font for the main header. This may not be appropriate for memos carrying serious content, but if the design is to be used for general information distribution, this approach will work perfectly well.*

TO:	Quality Assurance Managers
FROM:	Joanne O'Mara, Matthew Cooper
SUBJECT:	Staff Appraisals
DATE:	07/21/09

Operations Department

Store signs

Signage carrying information such as the opening times of a store must broadcast its content loud and clear to customers. There's nothing worse than turning up to start your shopping 10 minutes after closing time! As well as providing important information about the store's operations, the signage that store owners display can also help convey a sense of the products within.

OPENING HOURS

MONDAY	9am–5pm
TUESDAY	9am–5pm
WEDNESDAY	10am–6pm
THURSDAY	10am–8pm
FRIDAY	9am–6pm
SATURDAY	9am–6pm
SUNDAY	11am–4pm

1

OPENING HOURS

MONDAY	9am–5pm
TUESDAY	9am–5pm
WEDNESDAY	10am–6pm
THURSDAY	10am–8pm
FRIDAY	9am–6pm
SATURDAY	9am–6pm
SUNDAY	11am–4pm

2

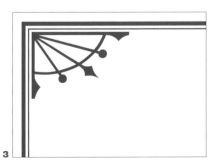

3

1 Prepare the text

Type up the correct list of opening times in an approximation of the layout you think you would like to follow. The version above is functional enough, but it doesn't have any particular visual style.

2 Add a border

If you want to draw attention to important information, adding a border or frame is a great way to help that along. Unless you want something highly decorative, don't get carried away with overly complicated borders, or the styling will overpower the information. A simple double-ruled border, as shown in our example, is a good choice. Borders are discussed in more detail on pages 064–065.

3 Add decorations

Adding further ornamentation can work really well if you want to create a particular feel for your signage, and can make it look a little more stylish. This decorative element is the "a" character from a symbol font named Adobe Wood Type Ornaments 1. (The same element for a right-hand corner is the "A.") A frame's corners attract the most attention, so adding detail to corners is particularly effective.

OPENING HOURS

MONDAY	9am–5pm
TUESDAY	9am–5pm
WEDNESDAY	10am–6pm
THURSDAY	10am–8pm
FRIDAY	9am–6pm
SATURDAY	9am–6pm
SUNDAY	11am–4pm

4

5

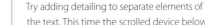

4 Finishing touches

Try adding detailing to separate elements of the text. This time the scrolled device below the titling is the "Q" from Adobe Wood Type Ornaments 2. Symbol fonts provide a great method for creating this type of decorative detailing without the need to draw it yourself. Note that we've also neatened the text up by aligning it on both sides of the column. This was achieved using a right indent tab (*see* Glossary).

5 Add color

The last thing to add is a little more color. Choose a combination that works well using the techniques we discussed on pages 074–081 and pick out one or two elements of the layout to finish off the design.

↓ *The finished piece in our example would look perfect in an antiques store or gift emporium.*

DONE

OPENING HOURS

MONDAY	9am–5pm
TUESDAY	9am–5pm
WEDNESDAY	10am–6pm
THURSDAY	10am–8pm
FRIDAY	9am–6pm
SATURDAY	9am–6pm
SUNDAY	11am–4pm

Menus

You may never need to design a menu, but the principles behind this type of design can be applied to any typographic list that requires a hierarchy in order to present the information clearly. The skills involved are of the kind that professional designers use all the time when undertaking creative projects.

Hot Drinks

Coffee	$3.00
Cappuccino	$5.00
Double espresso	$5.00
Latte	$5.00
Mocha	$5.00
Hot tea	$4.00
Iced Tea	$4.00

1

1 First decisions

Before you begin the full layout process, make some basic decisions about typefaces, type weights, and type sizes in order to establish how your typographic hierarchy will work.

Frittata $12.00

with artichoke hearts, roasted tomatoes, rosemary potatoes, fresh basil, chorizo, niçoise olives, and Parmesan cheese

2

2 Dish descriptions

Next, take a look at any entries that take up more than one line and decide how you'll handle the information. We've placed the price in bold next to the dish, with the description set in a lighter weight beneath. This helps each dish to stand out in the longer listing.

3 Extra information

If any dishes have extra side-order options, pick that information out with italics or indented paragraphs. Here, the choices of beverage are indented by 3mm (1/8in).

3

Good Start Breakfast $10.00

Oatmeal or cereal with strawberries
and bananas
   choose from:
   Raisin Bran, Corn Flakes,
   Fruit Loops, Special K*, Rice Krispies,
   apricot-almond granola, or oatmeal
   accompanied by:
   coffee, hot tea, or iced tea

4 Design a logo

Every type of business benefits from having its own logo—cafés are no exception. We've chosen a script font called Radio which has a friendly and informal feel. This welcoming feel comes through in the logo, which is essential for a business such as a café.

4

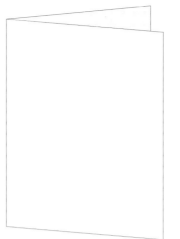

5 **Folding options**

There are several basic folding options for this type of design project. Above, from left to right, we have a simple two-sided sheet, followed by a four-page menu formed with a single fold, and finally a concertina fold, giving us six pages in total. The size of each page is dependent on the overall size of the original paper stock.

6 **Arrange the pages**

You'll need to arrange your pages in "printer's pairs" so that they print in the correct order, on both sides of the paper. A four-page menu is very easy to work out—just make sure that the front and back covers are arranged as shown on the right.

7 **Design a grid**

Even for simple projects such as this, our advice is, always design a basic grid (*see* pages 058–061). In this case we'll use a two-column grid with even margins at the sides and base of the pages. The top margin has been made slightly wider so we can incorporate our logo and menu title as part of the final layout.

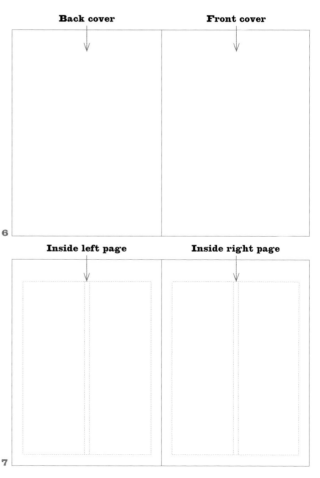

Back cover   Front cover

Inside left page   Inside right page

Annie's Café

Frittata $12.00
with artichoke hearts, roasted tomatoes, rosemary potatoes, fresh basil, chorizo, niçoise olives, and Parmesan cheese

Carb Conscious Frittata $12.00
Egg or egg-white omelet with country ham, apple-smoked bacon, cheddar cheese, and ruby-red onions

Eggs Benedict $13.00
Traditional: poached eggs, toasted English muffin, rotisserie ham, and hollandaise; served with potatoes
Florentine: poached eggs, toasted English muffin, spinach, tomato, and hollandaise; served with potatoes

Breakfast Croissant $13.00
Scrambled eggs, ham, cheddar cheese; served with potatoes

From the Griddle $9.00
All served with warm maple syrup and whipped vanilla butter:
Brown sugar waffle
Buttermilk pancakes
  choose from:
  mixed berries, plain, or bananas
Vanilla French toast
  topped with fresh bananas

Breakfast Buffet $18.00
Includes your choice of:
Omelets, waffles, French toast, eggs, bacon, breakfast potatoes, oatmeal, fruit, yogurts, pastries, juice, and coffee

Bakery Breakfast $8.00
Fresh morning bread and pastries with sweet cream butter and preserve
  choose from:
  muffin, croissant, or Danish
  accompanied by:
  coffee, hot tea, or iced tea

All-American Breakfast $13.00
2 eggs prepared your style
with potatoes and your choice
of the following:
Eggs: scrambled (well or soft), over (easy, medium, hard), sunny-side up, 3-minute, poached (easy, medium, hard), coddled
Meat: apple-smoked bacon, sausage links, sausage patties, spicy breakfast sausage, rotisserie ham
Toast: white, wholegrain, raisin, sourdough, rye, bagel
Drink: coffee, hot tea, iced tea

Good Start Breakfast $10.00
Oatmeal or cereal with strawberries and bananas
  choose from:
  Raisin Bran, Corn Flakes, Fruit Loops, Special K*, Rice Krispies, apricot-almond granola, or oatmeal
  accompanied by:
  coffee, hot tea, or iced tea

Sunshine Breakfast

Omelets $13.00

All omelets are served with potatoes and your choice of toast

California: egg whites, spinach, broccoli, avocado

Western: ham, cheddar cheese, peppers

Vegetarian: mushrooms, asparagus, tomatoes, artichokes

Spanish: chorizo, jalapeños, cheddar cheese, pico de gallo

Alpine: spinach, mushrooms, ham, goat cheese

Side Orders

Apricot-almond granola with yogurt or soy milk	$6.00
Cold cereal with milk	$5.00
Sausage links, sausage patties, apple-smoked bacon, spicy breakfast sausage, rotisserie ham	$4.00
Breakfast potatoes	$3.00
Toast (white, wholegrain, sourdough, raisin, rye)	$3.00
Bagel (plain, sesame, onion)	$3.00
Muffin	$3.00
Fresh berries and yogurt	$6.00
Fresh fruit	$5.00

Freshly squeezed juices $4.00

Orange
Grapefruit
Apple
Tomato
White cranberry
Pineapple

Smoothies $5.00

Apple and kiwi
Mango, orange, and pineapple
Blueberry and banana
Apple, banana, and coconut
Strawberry and banana

Hot drinks

Coffee	$3.00
Cappuccino	$5.00
Double espresso	$5.00
Latte	$5.00
Mocha	$5.00
Hot tea	$4.00
Iced Tea	$4.00

← *Here we have the finished layout for the interior of our menu. As you can see, we've incorporated our café's logo at the top to remind our customers where they are, and each individual dish is clearly picked out using the typographical hierarchy we've developed. The side orders and drinks are grouped together at the end of the listing as these tend to be the last things that customers choose when ordering.*

DONE

Breakfast Mon–Sun 6:30am–10:30am
Lunch Mon–Sun 11:30am–3:00pm
Dinner Sun–Thurs 5:30pm–10:30pm
Fri–Sat seating until 11:00pm

Gratuity of 18% added to parties of eight or more

Call 619.446.6088 for reservations and information
56 Montgomery Street, San Diego, CA 92101

DONE

Annie's Café

Sunshine Breakfast

← To finish off the project we needed a design for the front and back covers of our menu. The logo has been developed further and now utilizes the silhouette of a coffee cup; a visual association trick that is often used in all kinds of logo design. Our breakfast menu is called the "Sunshine Breakfast," so we've chosen an image of a fried egg with a big yellow yolk which looks rather like a rising sun.

Invitations

The design of invitations to events such as parties and weddings is normally driven very much by the personal tastes of the client, so professional designers must pay particular attention to their customers' requirements for this kind of project. As your own client, you're in the perfect position to create exactly what you want.

1 Choose a format

The easiest solution is a straightforward card printed on either one or two sides. If you choose this option, go for a format that will fit a standard-sized envelope or you'll incur unnecessary expense. Our solution is a neat way to avoid the need for an envelope: the invitation folds into itself for mailing out to guests. The diagrams to the right show how the invitation is made from one piece of card.

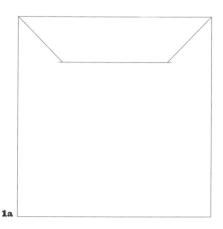

1a

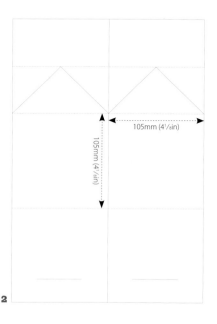

1b

105mm (4¹/₈in)

105mm (4¹/₈in)

2

2 Make a template

We've chosen dimensions that allow us to make two invitations from an A4 sheet of card, a standard size for inkjet printers. In the US, the equivalent standard is 8¹/₂ × 11in, also known as "letter." When folded, the invitation will be 105mm (4¹/₈in) square. Draw a template to help you get the folds and text in the right positions.

3 Choose your stock

You'll need to choose a good-quality card for this kind of project. It should be sturdy enough to withstand the battering it will get in the mail, but not so thick that it is difficult to fold cleanly. It also needs to be of a weight that your inkjet can cope with, so check the printer's specifications to ensure you don't use a stock that could stick and cause damage.

MR. AND MRS. F. PARKER
REQUEST THE HONOR OF YOUR PRESENCE
AT THE MARRIAGE OF THEIR DAUGHTER

Emma Louise Parker

MR. AND MRS. F. PARKER
REQUEST THE HONOR OF YOUR PRESENCE
AT THE MARRIAGE OF THEIR DAUGHTER

Emma Louise Parker
TO
James Alexander Sutton

ON SATURDAY SEPTEMBER 19
AT HAMPSHIRE HOUSE
BEACON ST, BOSTON, MA 02108

4 Choose the main font

Choose a principal font that is easy to read as the information set in this font is very important. It would be a disaster if any guests arrived at the wrong address or on the wrong date. Highly decorative or stylized fonts are not always very legible. We've chosen Adobe Caslon small caps.

5 Choose a stylized font

For the names, or other highlighted details, you can use a decorative font. This elaborate script font, Balmoral, isn't difficult to read, but the invitation would look a little over-the-top if all the text were set in it. The mix of fonts gives us a much more elegant and stylish solution.

6 Bringing it together

This combination of fonts is working well without looking overly decorative or fussy. A degree of typographic restraint could be considered a hallmark of a professionally designed invitation. It's important to get the spacing between the blocks of type right in order to achieve a well-proportioned visual grouping, so ensure that a little space is added above and below the names to provide some visual emphasis.

MR. AND MRS. F. PARKER
REQUEST THE HONOR OF YOUR PRESENCE
AT THE MARRIAGE OF THEIR DAUGHTER

Emma Louise Parker

TO

James Alexander Sutton

ON SATURDAY SEPTEMBER 19
AT HAMPSHIRE HOUSE
BEACON ST, BOSTON, MA 02108

CEREMONY COMMENCES AT 1:00PM

PLEASE CONFIRM THAT YOU ARE ABLE TO ATTEND
E-MAIL FRANK.PARKER@FAMILYPARKER.COM

7

7 Position your text

After adding any additional information, position the text group centrally within the square that will be covered when the card is folded in on itself. Move the group slightly nearer the top of the square, or the text will appear too close to the lower edge.

JACK AND CLAIRE PORTINARI
65 NEW ENGLAND ST
BOSTON
MA 02108

8 Add the addresses

The final requirement is the addition of the mailing address to the reverse side of each invitation. The smartest way to achieve this is to typeset the address in the same font for each individual invitation, and feed the card through your inkjet a second time, but you must do this before you trim and fold the cards or the type will not line up correctly. (Refer to the cutting and folding techniques discussed on pages 026–029 for tips on best practice.) If you'd rather add a personal touch, you can always opt to handwrite the addresses after trimming out the cards.

8

→ *Our final invitation is both elegant and practical. The folding design means there is no need to use envelopes to mail out the invitations. The addition of a small adhesive sticker to ensure the flap remains closed may be advisable.*

MR. AND MRS. F. PARKER
REQUEST THE HONOR OF YOUR PRESENCE
AT THE MARRIAGE OF THEIR DAUGHTER

Emma Louise Parker
TO
James Alexander Sutton

ON SATURDAY SEPTEMBER 19
AT HAMPSHIRE HOUSE
BEACON ST, BOSTON, MA 02108

CEREMONY COMMENCES AT 1:00PM

PLEASE CONFIRM THAT YOU ARE ABLE TO ATTEND
E-MAIL FRANK.PARKER@FAMILYPARKER.COM

If you dare, you are invited
to celebrate the night of the dead
in the village of the damned
at Nicky's

HALLOWE'EN
PARTY

7.30pm
Friday 31st October

21 Lower Lane, Alfriston, BN62 5X2
Telephone 01323 654321
nicky@gmail.com

← *An invitation to a Hallowe'en party is about as far from a wedding invitation as one can get, and the visual here illustrates that. The colors and the styling evoke the spooky feeling my friend wanted when she asked if I would put together an invite for her party. To save some time I purchased the background illustration online at istockhoto.com, and the font is the fantastically named Bleeding Cowboys.*

Business stationery

The professional appearance of a business's stationery will always set it apart from its competitors. A well-designed business card or letterhead projects a positive message to customers, and indicates that the owners of the business are serious about their company and its product. This example describes our take on the design of an electrician's logo and stationery.

1 Brainstorm concepts

To get the ball rolling with a concept for your logo, write down as many things as you can think of that are associated with the type of business you're designing for. Professional designers often keep a thesaurus to hand and use word association as part of this process.

2 Develop a visual concept

Our electrician's first name is Edward, and the "E" has reminded us of the pins of an Australian electric plug. This provides us with our visual concept which we can now develop further.

3 Combine the shapes

Our next move combines the three "prongs" of the plug with a vertical rectangle. Notice that the prongs are now a little thinner, are evenly spaced, and have moved closer together to form a combined shape which resembles a regular plug more closely.

4 Add more shapes

The whole of the logo we've planned is constructed of simple geometric shapes, making it very easy to draw and assemble into the final form. The smaller line drawing above shows how the shapes overlap and combine to provide the outline of our plug. When these shapes are filled with a solid area of color, the overlaps can be adjusted as required until the overall shape looks just right.

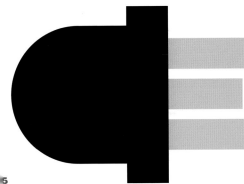

5 Finishing touches

Now is the time to begin thinking about how color can add to the look and feel of your logo. Once again, use the techniques you learned about in the section on color harmony and choose combinations of colors that work well together and feel right for the subject.

DONE

↗ Once you've finalized the shape of the logo you can add any elements you feel will enhance the design further, such as the length of cable and the repeated "E."

EDWARD RICHARDSON
6 ELECTRICIAN

6 Choose a font

When designing any kind of stationery, the font you choose to work with can be either something neutral, for example, Helvetica, or something that fits visually with the activities of the person or company you are designing for. The font we've chosen for our project, AFPAN, has an interesting industrial quality to it which works nicely.

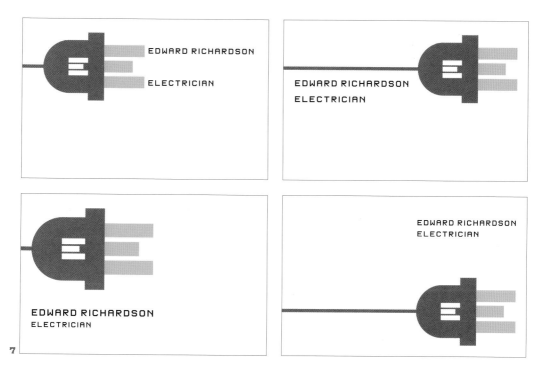

7 Position the logo

Experiment with the positioning of the logo and company name, using the rules we discussed throughout Chapter 2. Of the four examples shown here, I'm leaning toward the one at bottom left as the scale of the logo and type feels comfortable within the overall area of the business card, and because there is room on the right for the all-important contact details. We've started with the business card for this example, but there's no set order for design: you could start with the letterhead, a compliments slip, or a mailing label.

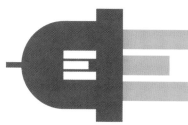

🔇 **(07) 4747 7762**
electric.edward@aol.com

16 Bogong St
Mount Isa
Qld 4825

EDWARD RICHARDSON
ELECTRICIAN

8 Add contact details

The contact details fit perfectly alongside the prongs of the logo, providing a neat visual balance to the card. Notice that the phone number and e-mail address are shown slightly larger than the postal details, as they are the most likely means by which an electrician's customers would get in touch.

9 Printing options

You could have a printer produce the final items of stationery for you, but it is possible to print your own as and when you need them if you have a good-quality inkjet at your disposal. This option provides the advantage of allowing you to change contact details instantly if you move to another address.

← *These cards were printed "DIY" using an ordinary inkjet capable of accepting a heavier paper stock suitable for this kind of application. Always check the specification of your printer before using heavyweight stock as a serious paper jam could cause irreparable damage to your printer.*

→ *The logo's power cord has been extended across the top of the letterhead to provide a natural position for the contact details. This is not breaking the visual consistency rule for the logo, as the main element of the design (the plug) has not changed. Note also that we've added discreet marks to the right edge of the letterhead, dividing the letterhead into three equal portions for accurate folding.*

℡ **(07) 4747 7762 //** *electric.edward@aol.com*
16 Bogong St, Mount Isa, Queensland 4825

EDWARD RICHARDSON
ELECTRICIAN

10

DONE

10 Other stationery items

The elements created for the business card can be used in different configurations for the letterhead, compliments slip, and so on. It is important to maintain consistency for the logo, but other items of text can be arranged according to the format of each stationery item.

Using fonts for logos

A logo for a company, or for an individual, doesn't have to include a pictorial element like the graphic plug we created for our fictitious electrician. It is possible to design a functional and attractive logo using only fonts, with maybe a rule or border thrown in for good measure. The examples below, business cards for an imagined professional consultant, manage to feel different primarily through the use of different fonts. Color also plays a part in this, but the fonts are what really create the different impressions.

Helen Waterhouse
Consultant

Tel: 04321 567039
E-mail: hejassociates@tbinternet.com

← Look at this card and decide for yourself what kind of company HEJ Associates could be. I see a card that could belong to a consultant for an engineering firm, or a transportation and courier company. The sans-serif font looks practical, dependable, and hardworking.

HEJ
ASSOCIATES

Helen Waterhouse
Consultant

Tel: 04321 567039
E-mail: hejassociates@tbinternet.com

← This card carries exactly the same information, but feels quite different. The serif font looks more serious and authoritative, and could belong to someone working for a firm of solicitors, or perhaps a financial institution. A simple change of font combined with a slightly more formal styling for the layout sends out a very different message.

Application forms

Forms are generally rather dull. Nobody likes the task of completing a form, and I am no exception. In fact, I would rather design a form than fill one out. However, if a form is well designed, simple to navigate through, and easy to use, the task is a far less onerous one.

1 Allow enough space

One of the most common mistakes made by inexperienced designers when laying out a form is not allowing enough space to write the required information. This example provides very little in the way of space for the address.

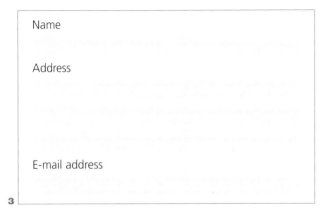

Name_____

Address_____

_____

1

2 Box it in

Tinted boxes are a neat way of designating space for writing as they encourage people to give only the required information. However, there still isn't enough space for an address in this revised example.

Name

Address

E-mail address

2

3 Improve the space

This third example is much improved in terms of the amount of space provided for the user to fill in their details. We've moved the labels above the boxes to allow them to be made wider, and we've provided three lines for the address details. Keep any colored tints as pale as possible (without making them so pale that they disappear), or the handwritten information will be difficult to read.

Name

Address

E-mail address

3

Name

Personal details

Name

4 Color the background

Here's an alternative treatment that solves the potential problem of writing on a colored tint box. We've swapped the tint from the box to the background so the user can write on white paper. This is the preferable design for a form as writing directly onto an unprinted surface is much easier, especially if the user is writing with anything other than a ballpoint pen.

Address

5

5 Label the sections

If there are distinct sections to your form, make sure you indicate that clearly through the use of a graphic device such as a border or tinted area, or by using a bolder font to provide a section heading.

Duration of Course

Type of Course (tick as appropriate)

full time   part time   evening

6

6 Add tick boxes

Wherever there are options from which to choose, tick boxes are the best way to indicate which option has been chosen. Always make sure that each label is clearly linked to its specific box by using proximity.

Accommodation (tick as appropriate)

I intend to stay in accommodation provided by the college

I intend to stay with a family who live nearby

I intend to stay in independent shared accommodation in the city

7

7 List options

You can also use tick boxes at the end of listed options, as shown above. Again, the key to the functionality of the tick boxes is to remove any ambiguity about which option has been chosen by the user. They don't have to be square either—try experimenting with circles, or whatever shapes you care to try out.

8 Tabular information

Using a table to present information is a bit like using a grid (*see* pages 058–061) to design a page in a brochure or book. A fixed cellular structure laid out in tabular form dictates where each item should be placed.

8

9

9 Design the tables

The type of information you need to represent will dictate the number of rows and columns you must create. Our example requires a table in which 12 general details can be listed and ticked where applicable.

10 Add the text

When adding text to a table, be as concise as possible in order to maximize use of the available space. To ensure that each item will fit into the given space, work out which is the longest, and set the column width to fit that. As you can see, the entries at bottom left do not fit, so the column width must be increased.

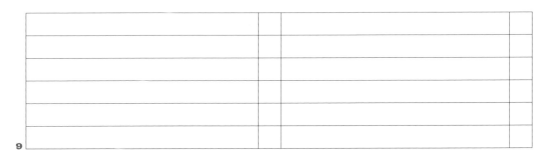

I am registered with a local doctor	I have taken a course here before	
I am registered with a local dentist	This is my first time at this college	
I have a grant to fund myself	I have lived in this city before	
I have a student loan to fund myself	I am new to this city	
I have a part-time job to fund myself	I have my own transport	
I am looking for a job to fund myself	I intend to use public transport	

10

→ *Here is the completed design for the application form. It's a relatively simple form by the standards of some you may encounter, but the principles we've described can be applied to other, far more complex layouts.*

Westbourne College

Registration and Enrollment form

DONE

Personal details

Name

Tel. No.

Address

Work Tel. No.

E-mail Address

Course details

Name of Course

Duration of Course

Start Date

Type of Course (tick as appropriate)

full time   part time   evening

Accommodation (tick as appropriate)

I intend to stay in accommodation provided by the college

I intend to stay with family who live nearby

I intend to stay in independent shared accommodation in the city

General details (tick as appropriate)

I am registered with a local doctor		I have taken a course here before	
I am registered with a local dentist		This is my first time at this college	
I have a grant to fund myself		I have lived in this city before	
I have a student loan to fund myself		I am new to this city	
I have a part-time job to fund myself		I have my own transport	
I am looking for a job to fund myself		I intend to use public transport	

Fees

Signature

I enclose a fee of _____ for:

a full year   one term   (tick as appropriate)

Advertisements

Whether you run your own business, are an employer or an employee, it's possible that at some point you'll be involved in the process of hiring someone. Getting the press advertisement right goes a long way to ensuring you get the right applicants for the position.

1 Begin the text

Start by thinking carefully about the main text, especially the job description, which must make clear all the relevant requirements. If you omit any important points, you may receive a lot of inappropriate applications.

2 Add contact details

Make sure the contact information is accurate and up-to-date, and be clear about whether or not an e-mailed application is acceptable: some people prefer a handwritten letter as part of a job application.

3 Begin the layout

Once you're sure you've got all the necessary text and graphics together, you can begin the design process. Double-check the size, which will be specified by the publication you've chosen to advertise with, and apply the techniques we've discussed for typographic hierarchy, emphasis, and structure. In our example, the job title is given maximum prominence to draw the viewer's eyes away from the other ads that will be wrestling for attention on the page. We've also changed the job description to a bullet-point list so that applicants can check off the requirements against their own qualifications or skills more easily. Finally, we've allowed some space to display the company logo at top left, which will also help to attract attention.

Agua Beauty Salons are looking for an

ASSISTANT BEAUTY THERAPIST

Relevant experience essential, and candidate must hold NVQ Level 4 or similar qualifications. A keen interest in Reflexology would be an advantage.

1

Agua Beauty Salons are looking for an

ASSISTANT BEAUTY THERAPIST

Relevant experience essential, and candidate must hold NVQ Level 4 or similar qualifications. A keen interest in Reflexology would be an advantage.

To apply, send your CV to:
Moira Jones, HR Manager, 9 Hobson Rd, Cambley, MN 56339
or e-mail: moirajones@aguasalons.com

2

logo   Agua Beauty Salons are looking for an

ASSISTANT BEAUTY THERAPIST

• Relevant experience essential
• Must hold NVQ Level 4 or similar qualifications
• Keen interest in Reflexology an advantage

To apply, send your CV to:
Moira Jones, HR Manager, 9 Hobson Rd, Cambley, MN 56339
or e-mail: *moirajones@aguasalons.com*

3

↑ When placed among other standardized small ads, our example stands out considerably, making it a much more effective advertising device.

→ Our finished layout has developed into a clean and attractive design which feels appropriate for the type of position being advertised. Adding the company logo gives the ad an increased visual punch, and the typographic hierarchy and styling ensure that all relevant information is both clear and easy to cross-reference. If you are advertising in more than one place, the addition of a reference number means you can track which publication the applicant has used.

DONE

agua

Agua Beauty Salons are looking for an

ASSISTANT BEAUTY THERAPIST

- Relevant experience essential
- Must hold NVQ Level 4 or similar qualifications
- Keen interest in Reflexology an advantage

To apply, send your CV to:
Moira Jones, HR Manager, 9 Hobson Rd, Cambley, MN 56339
or e-mail: *moirajones@aguasalons.com*
Please quote reference 23-7-GDN in your covering letter

Festival banners

Large, colorful banners are extremely eye-catching, and are one of the best ways to publicize events of all kinds. What's more, they're incredibly flexible and can be hung in many different types of location for maximum effect and exposure.

1

1 Pick your dimensions

Banners are usually long and narrow, and this can pose one or two problems for professional as well as untrained designers. Images will need to be cropped judiciously, and careful consideration must be given to the content in order to achieve a pleasing fit.

2 Position the type

Any type that needs to be included must be sized and laid out carefully to ensure that it all fits successfully, particularly if you have to deal with long words over the narrow measure. In our example, the main headline type fits well and the space-to-type ratio looks comfortable.

Summer Festival
21st–24th August
Preston Park

Summer Festival
21st–24th August
Preston Park

Summer Festival
21st–24th August
Preston Park

2

3

4

3 Readability

In the first example the position of the type means the banner may be difficult to read if it is displayed a lot higher than ground level. Positioning the type in the middle of the banner would cover most eventualities, but the addition of an image may not allow the type to be centered.

4 The safe option

If you're not sure where your banner will be displayed, or at what height it will be hung, placing the type at the bottom would be the safest option. If your chosen image has a lot of detail in the lower portion that creates readability issues, you can simply add a colored (or plain white) panel which will accommodate the type.

5 Source an image

Image libraries, which we discussed back in Chapter 1, are a great place to search for images for this kind of project, but don't forget to go over your own collection of photographs if you have one. These kinds of images are worth collecting for possible future use, so if you ever happen across a fortunate photo opportunity, be sure to get snapping.

5

6 Crop for impact

Cropping into a smaller portion of your chosen photograph may yield a much more dynamic image for your banner design. You may prefer to select the area by cutting a hole in a piece of card that is the same proportion as the banner and moving this over the image. You can also use two L-shaped pieces of black card held at right angles to choose the best crop. This was the technique used by professional photographers and designers before the advent of computers and Adobe Photoshop.

6

7a   7b   7c   7d

7 Composition

The four images we've picked for our project are all potentially suitable for use in the design of our banner advertising a summer festival.

(a) The colors in this image are great, but tulips are also spring-flowering so the image is less suitable for a summer festival.

(b) This image is also nicely colorful, but the type doesn't work as well as in the others because there is no clear area in which to position it.

(c) While beautifully understated, the grass on its own doesn't quite capture the full feeling of summer. We need some flowers too.

(d) What better flower to do that than a carpet of pretty daisies? The image is also nicely proportioned in terms of the amount of visible sky, with a clear area for the type. This is the image we'll choose to carry forward for our final design.

8 Get it printed

This is obviously too big a job for your home printer, so shop around for a local company that can handle this type of work. You'll find there is a fairly wide range of materials that can be used for such a project, from fabrics and canvas to waterproof plastics, which are very hardwearing and can be used many times over. If you do want to reuse your banner, don't add specific dates as these will almost definitely change from one year to the next.

DONE

↓ → *There are various ways in which banners can be displayed. Check the options available before you get your banners printed and finished, as some materials are likely to be better suited to certain hanging options than others.*

Summer Festival

21st–24th August
Preston Park

a

CD & DVD packaging

The prospect of designing a record cover or DVD package is one of the prime motives for people embarking on a career in graphic design. Designing for the music and entertainment industry, or simply for a friend's (or your own) band, is a very rewarding experience creatively.

1 Select the image

The greatest designs for album covers often begin with a striking image. This cool-looking tower, photographed by Jane, is in Berlin, Germany, so it's a good choice for our imaginary band Channel Hoppers, and the imagery works with the proposed name for the album, *Sunspot Cycle*.

1

2

2 Choose crop & layout

A standard CD wallet (not a jewel case, but a simple card case) measures 127 × 127mm (5 × 5in), so our portrait-shaped image needs to be cropped to fit the square format. There is some interesting detail at the top of the image where you can just see some small red lights, and the design will benefit from the retention of that detail, so we'll crop from the bottom of the image to square it up.

3 Add the text

Initially, the inclination is to add the band name and album title to the center of the image area, on either side of the tower. While this balances out visually, the type doesn't read well. The album could be called *Sunspot Channel*, and be by a band called the Cycle Hoppers. We need to rethink this layout.

4 Split the text

This works much better. Moving the album title away from the band name creates the right amount of separation, works well visually, and the interaction of the title with those red light details I mentioned earlier is very effective.

3

➜ *This is the finished design for the front face of the album cover. Its strength is its simplicity, and the image provides us with a striking and memorable cover that will resonate with the band's fans.*

4

5 Design the back

Once again, an evocative image is a great place to start. This one works because it's intriguing—it's more interesting than the typical "band members staring into lens" imagery that often appears on album covers.

6 Add the text

Another useful aspect of this shot is the area of empty sky at the top. It's an ideal position for the band name, album title, and track listing to be placed. When choosing images for a project, always think about where type or additional graphics can be positioned successfully.

CHANNEL HOPPERS
SUNSPOT CYCLE

1. Lucky ones
2. Timber
3. Ship to shore
4. Family picnic
5. Remote control

6. Citizen radio
7. Skydiver
8. Apples and pears
9. Your choice

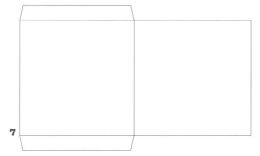

7 Create a wallet template

If you want to handmake the CD wallets, base your template on the diagram here. The front and back faces are 127 × 127mm (5 × 5in), and the flaps on the edges of the front cover hold everything together. I recommend double-sided tape to fasten the wallet.

8 Lay out the artwork

Make sure the front and back artwork are positioned as shown here.

→ The final CD wallet.

SUNSPOT CYCLE

CHANNEL HOPPERS

9

9 The DVD cover

Our band is also releasing a DVD of its latest European tour, and the design of the packaging ties in with the CD cover. It's fortunate that the format of our original image is portrait, as standard DVD packaging artwork measures 183 x 130mm (5 x 7in).

10 The back cover

We're able to utilize the same basic layout as the CD cover with some adjustment to the crop of the original shot. The portrait crop is actually an improvement on the CD cover as the increased areas of foreground and sky give the image a more dynamic feel.

11 The spine

A standard DVD pack has a 13mm (½in) spine, so that must be designed as an extra. A severe crop of the front-cover image works well, and the type sits neatly on the image. Spines are often ignored and "under designed," which is a wasted opportunity as when DVDs are racked up on a shelf in a store, or even at home on a bookcase, the spine is the only part of the cover that is visible.

CHANNEL HOPPERS
SUNSPOT CYCLE

1. Lucky ones
2. Timber
3. Ship to shore
4. Family time
5. Remote control
6. Citizen radio
7. Skydiver
8. Apples and pears
9. Your choice

10

Concert posters & fliers

Concert posters and fliers are a permanent fixture in most people's surroundings, particularly if they live in a city or town. If the band has a contract with a label, their publicity material will be produced by professional marketing and design people, but the vast majority of bands design their own. A large dose of individuality will help your poster or flyer stand out in a crowded market.

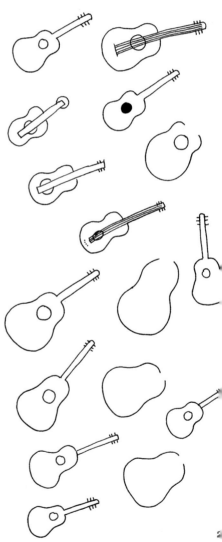

1 Create a character

Instead of a straight photographic approach for our poster and flier content, we've decided to create an illustrated character to represent the music of the band.

2 Sketch your ideas

After sketching some alternative characters, think about adding an instrument. Leader's music is guitar-led, so a guitarist is the natural choice for our character. Because this is a cartoon-style character, our drawing skills don't have to be perfect.

3

4

3 Combine the elements

Once you've got a version of the character and instrument you like, combine them in a single drawing. You can do this with a computer and scanner, or by hand, using a lightbox and some layout or tracing paper.

4 The finished character

Here he is. Our lead singer is transformed into a cartoon character that can be used to give both the poster and the flier a unique visual identity that people will remember.

Leader

Friday 7th March 2009
Cella Bar @ Sanctuary
Brunswick St
Doors 8.00pm
Onstage 8.15pm
$6 / $5 conc.

www.myspace.com/themightyleader

5

5 The concert information

Use the rules of typographic emphasis and hierarchy that we discussed in Chapter 2 when setting the information about the venue and concert timings.

6

6 The poster design

Combine your type and illustration using the grouping techniques we covered on pages 046–049. Our character looks too small here, and isn't positioned well against the type.

Leader

**www.myspace.com/
themightyleader**

Friday 7th March 2009
Cella Bar @ Sanctuary
Brunswick St
Doors 8.00pm
Onstage 8.15pm
$6 / $5 conc.

7

8

7 Adjust the layout

This version is a big improvement on the previous example. The space is used in a more dynamic way, and the character has much more visual impact. This final poster utilizes all the techniques of grouping, hierarchy, emphasis, and alignment that we've covered previously.

8 Color the background

To build up the visual impact even further, consider using a brightly colored paper stock for printing or photocopying. The pink and yellow stocks are rather more successful than the darker green example, which doesn't allow the black line work of the illustration to stand out strongly.

→ *The final poster, which looks suitably arresting and is full of visual impact.*

9

9 Display sites

When choosing where to display your posters, try to pick sites that have a background color or texture that will work *with* the poster rather than *against* it. Also, try to find sites that are legal, and where the poster won't be ripped down or damaged before it has been seen by as many people as possible.

10 Upload the poster

If you have a website or a page on a public service such as MySpace, save your poster in a suitable file format such as a JPEG, then upload it to the Internet for some extra publicity. Sites such as MySpace are highly automated so you don't require any in-depth knowledge of web design in order to create your own pages.

DONE

← *The poster and flier can double up so you don't need to design an extra item. Simply reduce the poster to whatever size you want the flier to be. To minimize costs and wastage, base the overall size around standard paper sizes so you can fit two or four fliers edge-to-edge on one sheet. This also makes the trimming process easier and quicker as there will be fewer cuts to make overall.*

Leader

www.myspace.com/ themightyleader

Friday 7th March
Cella Bar @ Sanctuary
Brunswick St
Doors 8.00pm
Onstage 8.15pm
$6 / $5 conc.

Sources of inspiration

There are always sources of inspiration that you can draw on for your graphic design projects. It takes some practice to know where to look, but in time you'll get the hang of it and the ideas will come to you much more easily.

The best places to start are, in a way, the most obvious. If you're working on a concert poster, for example, think about the name of the band or artist, think of associated imagery, and look at things like album titles or tour venues.

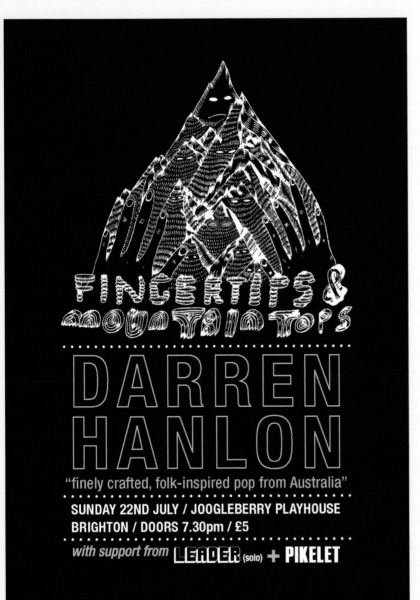

← This striking poster for Darren Hanlon's tour relies on strong typography and correctly gauged typographic emphasis, but the illustration also provides a great visual impact. Hanlon's album Fingertips & Mountaintops was the inspiration here.

Rubber stamps

Rubber stamps are incredibly flexible as, once you've designed a stamp and had it manufactured, you can use it over and over again, in as many different ways as you can think of. Our fictitious mobile disco needs a rubber stamp that can be used to mark the back of customers' hands when they arrive at an event.

1 Consider your logo

Gary Peacock's main logo is a DJ dog which can be adapted for all kinds of themed events, as shown in the sample fliers above. However, the design is too complex to adapt for a rubber stamp—this would benefit from a much simpler graphic device.

2 Associated shapes

To maintain the link with the dog in Gary's logo, we've come up with the idea of using a paw print for our stamp.

3 Refine the shape

The straightforward circles used in the design of the first option work well, but we've decided to experiment to see if a more interesting visual grouping can be achieved. Substituting an oval shape for the larger circle opens up possibilities for the placement of some type.

4 Add type

There isn't room to add the full title of the business here, so we'll just use the initials. This design is working well, but it's looking a little too unadventurous at the moment.

5 Adjust the type

Arranging the type in a square, as shown in step 5, is stronger visually. We could stop here, but there's still room for further development and experimentation.

6 Change the angle

We've decided to try rotating the paw print by 45° in a clockwise direction, and we're happier with the result. However, the rotation has necessitated a reduction in the type size to allow it to fit within the oval shape, which is not ideal.

7 Finalize the shape

The solution is to revert to the circular shape we used in our first visual. The rotation has provided us with a more dynamic visual, and the type size can be brought back up again. The idea has now developed enough for us to order our stamp.

8 Source the manufacturer

Our stamp must be small enough to fit on the back of someone's hand, but large enough not to fill in and lose its form when stamped. The artwork on the right is a pretty good size for this application. You will also need to check with your chosen manufacturer to make sure this is an available sizing option, as something that isn't a standard size may well cost more. To find a suitable supplier, simply go online and search for "rubber stamp manufacturer." If you can use someone in your area that's always a good thing, but most suppliers accept artwork via e-mail and will mail you your stamp within a few days.

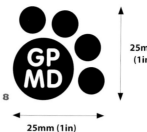

25mm (1in)

25mm (1in)

8

→ *Don't restrict yourself to one color when using your stamps, source as many alternative colors as you can for different events or occasions.*

DONE

→ *The finished stamp, and the applied design being used as intended.*

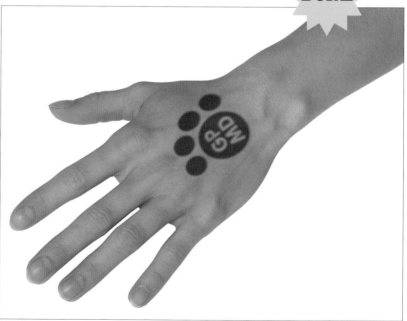

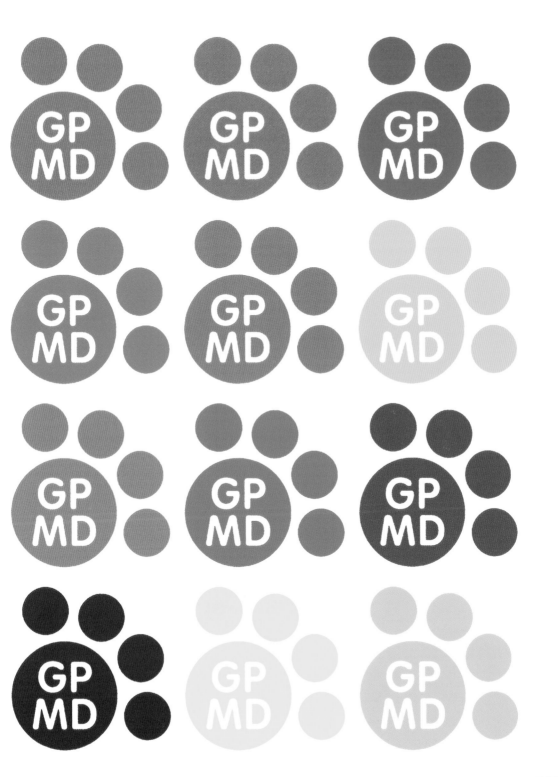

Event T-shirts

Designing and producing your own T-shirts for an event you're involved in is terrific fun, and it's not as difficult as it may seem. There are plenty of good-quality products that allow you to transfer your designs to a T-shirt, and if you want to produce more than one shirt, there are plenty of companies advertising online that will print them for you at surprisingly reasonable rates.

1 Create your text

The best T-shirts are built around a clear and concise message or statement, so bear that in mind when you're deciding how much text to include. Our advice is to keep text to a minimum—say only what you need to say about the event.

2 Categorize the event

If the event you're designing the shirt for is a regular fixture, remember to link the shirt to the particular occasion. The simplest way to do this is to add the date; if it's an annual event, just add the year.

1 Sydney to Melbourne Cycle Race

2 Sydney to Melbourne
CYCLE RACE 2009

3 2009

3 Consider a logo

Seeing the date written out has given us an idea for a logo. The double zero in "2009" could represent the wheels of a bicycle, so we've substituted the zeros from the chosen font, which is called Blender Bold, with two circles.

4 Create a graphic

A bicycle has a very distinct shape which isn't too difficult to draw. When you attempt to create a graphic representation of any object for this kind of use, always simplify the drawing. In this example we haven't included pedals, spokes, or other smaller details, but it is still unmistakably a road-race-style bicycle.

4

5 Create the logo

Combining the typographic and graphic elements gives us our event logo. The addition of a second color gives the logo some extra punch and helps the year stand out more.

6 Position the logo

The next decision concerns the sizing and placement of your graphics. The obvious place to position a design is right in the center of the chest area. This will maximize the space and allow you to make the logo as large as possible, but there are interesting alternatives to consider.

7 Small and off-center

Think about the possibilities of placing your graphics off-center, and at a smaller size. As there are no other graphics planned for this shirt, the smaller size will not stop the logo standing out.

8 Sleeve or side

You could also use the area on the sleeve to print all or even part of the logo. Perhaps you could use just a part of the logo, say the date, on the sleeve, then repeat the logo so it wraps around the side of the shirt. Try out as many options as you can think of in order to achieve the most interesting design.

5 **Sydney to Melbourne Cycle Race**

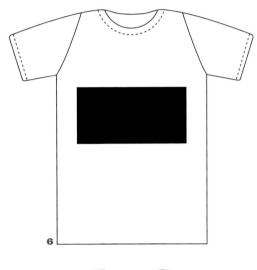

6

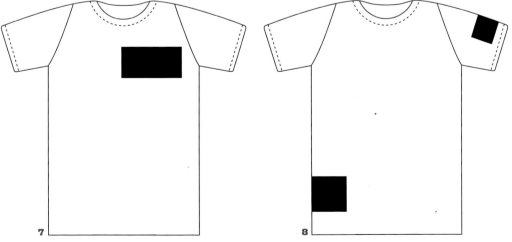

7

8

DONE

2OO9
Sydney to Melbourne Cycle Race

Front

↑ ↗ *For our final shirt design, we decided to position the main logo slightly off-center and on the right side of the chest area. This balances up nicely with a large graphic created to represent the route of the race from Sydney to Melbourne,* *including the staging posts, that wraps around from the back to the front of the shirt. As the graphic is purely decorative, there is no need to add any explanatory text.*

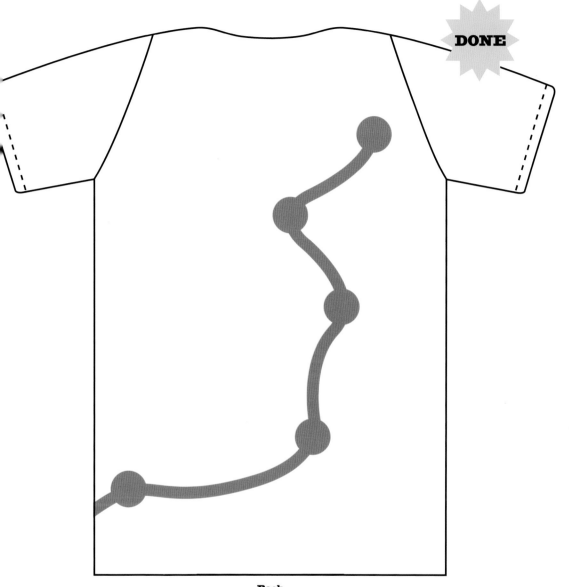

DONE

Back

Tags & labels

The process of designing a good tag or label should always start with a good hard look at the item upon which the tag or label will be attached. Sounds obvious, I know, but it's surprising how often one comes across designs that have been given a generic treatment, without any real consideration of the end use. Our project is based around an imagined fashion boutique.

1 Create a template

We're keeping it simple once again, and have designed a basic label shape that can be easily cut out by hand if mass-production isn't the order of the day. There are no difficult curves to follow, and the hole in the top can be punched through with an office hole punch.

2 Position the text

We've experimented with the position of the boutique logo, bearing in mind that we may need to add information to the tag, such as sizing information or price. The options with the type furthest away from the punched hole look to be the best choices so far.

1

2

3 Choose the colors

Our store is quite sophisticated (naturally!), and the tag colors need to reflect that. The color range above is certainly attractive, but it is more suitable for a bolder sales concept.

4 The paler option

This range uses the same basic colors but the strength of the tints has been reduced by 60%. The colors are now too weak and lack the impact and presence needed for this kind of tag.

5 The middle ground

These look just right for our store. The colors are strong, but not too bright, and the desired feeling of sophistication has been achieved.

Note that we swapped the original red for turquoise, as the quality of the red is lost in tints. This tint of turquoise is much more in keeping with the family of colors we have.

6 Add imagery

We're going to introduce some imagery that reflects the quality of the products carried by the boutique. The blossom on this tree creates a wonderful texture for the background, and as it is black-and-white, the whole range of colors can be applied to different tags.

6

7 Combine black-and-white with color

An image that combines a single color with black is called a duotone. The color shows through wherever there are no areas of black, and the result is a black-and-blue image, a black-and-green image, and so on.

7

8 Legibility

Adding the boutique logo to the tag after the duotone image has been applied creates a legibility problem, which is particularly bad with darker colors. Our solution is to introduce a black panel with white text on the bottom half of the tag, which solves the legibility issue for all possible combinations of color.

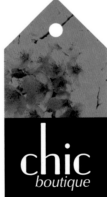

8

↓ Our final tag design can be used for all clothing ranges carried in the store, and each different clothing size has been allocated a different color tag. This makes choosing the correct size garment easy for the customers. If they are, say, a size 14, all they need do is search for purple tags when browsing the rails. Tags such as this form an important part of the identity of a retailer, so if you have a store of your own selling a particular kind of product, think carefully about the key features of that product, or think of the particular ambience you wish to create for the store, and that will give you your starting point.

DONE

Badges & pins

Designing and making your own badges can be terrific fun—the sky is the limit in terms of what you can do. Badges are extremely collectible, and can be used to promote anything from your favorite band to the next President of the United States.

1 Create the artwork template

Badges and pins are made to standard sizes as specialist badgemaking equipment dictates. Anything is possible, but as a nonprofessional badgemaker you should design to standard diameters. In Europe these are 25, 32, 38, and 55mm; in the US, 1, 1¼, 1½, and 2¼in. We have given decimal fractions for the Imperial measurements in the templates below, as these are what is used in software applications, and we've included only one set of templates as the differences between the metric and Imperial sizes are negligible.

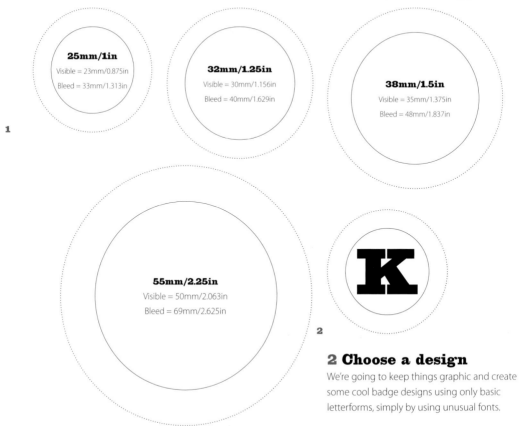

25mm/1in
Visible = 23mm/0.875in
Bleed = 33mm/1.313in

1

32mm/1.25in
Visible = 30mm/1.156in
Bleed = 40mm/1.629in

38mm/1.5in
Visible = 35mm/1.375in
Bleed = 48mm/1.837in

55mm/2.25in
Visible = 50mm/2.063in
Bleed = 69mm/2.625in

K

2

2 Choose a design

We're going to keep things graphic and create some cool badge designs using only basic letterforms, simply by using unusual fonts.

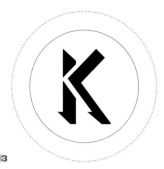

3 Select your fonts

Here's your chance to use as big a range of fonts as you like, without any real concerns about whether or not the style is right for your project. Just go wild and use whatever you like the look of. From left to right, these fonts are named Umbra, Rosewood, and Shababa.

4 Choose your colors

Again, choose whatever colors you want, and apply color to the fonts and the backgrounds. We've labeled each badge with the colors we've chosen, broken down into their CMYK components (*see* page 076). The extra fonts we've used are (bottom row, from left): VMR Shadow, OptiMorgan 3, and Princetown.

Bkgd: 000/085/085/000
Letter: 000/000/000/000

Bkgd: 100/000/015/000
Letter: 100/100/000/000

Bkgd: 050/000/100/000
Letter: 000/000/000/100

Bkgd: 095/000/070/000
Letter: 000/015/100/000

Bkgd: 035/075/000/000
Letter: 000/030/000/000

Bkgd: 000/015/100/000
Letter: 000/085/085/000

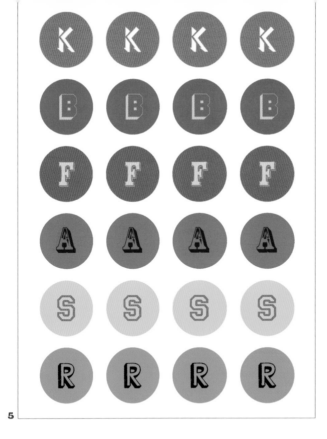

5

5 Save paper

When you print out the artwork for your badges, try to be as economical as you can with your paper, making sure there is enough space between the badges to cut each one out easily. It'll keep your costs down, and you'll be doing your bit for the environment too.

6 Cut the circles

Invest in a circle cutter if you want to cut perfect circles. A dedicated piece of kit like this makes an otherwise difficult task a breeze, and will save you lots of time and wasted printouts.

6

7 Manufacturing

To make perfect badges you will need to obtain a badge-making machine. The artwork and badge-making supplies, steel or plastic, are placed in the machine, and the handle is depressed to form the finished badge. Machine designs vary (the model illustrated here is a fairly high-end steel model), but most are fairly inexpensive. If you are serious about your badge making, invest in the best quality that your budget will allow.

DONE

← *The badges, trimmed, finished and ready to go.*

Giftwrap

There are thousands of different giftwraps available from retailers with designs that are appropriate for all manner of events. However, if you really want to personalize a gift, what better way to do it than to design your own giftwrap? This project shows you how to use simple shapes and color combinations to form repeat patterns.

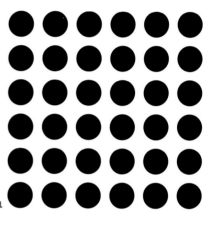

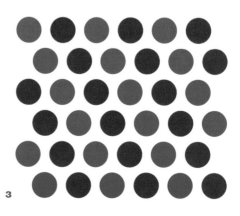

1 Uniform alignment

Rows and columns of a simple repeated shape can look OK, but the arrangement is a little dull and unadventurous. However, this provides us with a good place from which to start working on a more interesting arrangement. The process of generating lots of identical shapes in this way is often referred to by design professionals as "step-and-repeat."

2 Offset the pattern

To achieve the offset pattern above, we've simply moved each alternate row along to the left so the centers of the circles on alternate rows are aligned. Immediately, the pattern looks much more interesting, and we've got something we can take further.

3 Add some color

We've taken alternate diagonals, which were created when we offset the pattern in step 2, and applied two complementary colors. Use the techniques we discuss on pages 072–081 to pick the best color combinations. If you wanted to you could apply several colors randomly for a more varied overall effect.

4 Find visual inspiration

Using simple geometric shapes is an excellent way to get started with your designs, but you can also take your visual inspiration from images that you've shot yourself, or found in books or magazines.

5 Patterns from images

Once you've found an interesting image to use for reference, you can either trace the shape on your PC with whatever drawing application you favor, or use traditional pen and paper. A lightbox will prove very useful if you prefer not to use a computer.

4

5

6 Step & repeat

Once you've created a basic single form, such as this repeat pattern inspired by the image of the windmill, you can use the same step-and-repeat techniques you applied to the circles to build up a complex pattern. You could also combine two or more different forms in your design if the general shapes of the forms are able to link together without creating awkward areas of trapped space.

6

7 Build the pattern

We think this particular pattern works well without the introduction of an alternative set of shapes, so we'll stick with a single repeating form. The circular outline of the basic form means it's fairly easy to arrange the pattern with the offset repeat.

8 Crop the edges

If you wish you can stop the pattern before it reaches the edges of the giftwrap and fill the areas at the edges of the paper with a flat color, or simply leave it as empty space. We've decided to run the pattern right up to the edge of the trim and crop off the overhanging parts of the design.

9 Experiment with color

When selecting color combinations, always try a few alternatives to ensure that you've chosen the most pleasing and successful combination for your design.

→ *And there you have it! A unique and personal giftwrap. If you need large sheets for bigger gifts and have created the design on a computer, ask your local print shop what they would charge to output the file on a large-format inkjet. The more sheets you print, the cheaper the unit cost will be. In general, the cost should not be prohibitively expensive.*

DONE

Photographic patterns

You don't have to stick to drawn shapes for interesting and exclusive giftwrap designs. If you have a camera capable of taking images that can be enlarged enough to print on large sheets, try creating patterns using physical objects. This can be great fun, and doesn't require a great deal of photographic knowledge to achieve.

← *You can use pretty much what you like to make photographic patterns. These images of candies and cherries make wonderfully colorful giftwrap.*

Graphic maps

Maps are one of the purest and, to my mind, most wonderful examples of graphic design you can find. They are among the oldest forms of graphic design too—a city plan found painted on a wall in Anatolia, Turkey, is believed to date from around 6000 BC! Anyone who has even a passing interest in graphic design should attempt to design a map as part of the development of their design skills.

1 Mapping styles

The highly developed Ordnance Survey (OS) or U.S. Geological Survey (USGS) cartography that we see in numerous maps and atlases provides the best possible reference for any mapping projects. Bear in mind that you cannot mimic the style of these maps as you would then be in breach of the copyright.

1

2 **Maps as diagrams**

Maps, effectively, are diagrams, and can be rendered in any combination of styles. This example, a street plan of an imagined city, demonstrates how illustration and information graphics can be combined in diagrammatic form to produce a very effective map.

2

3

3 **Key features**

We are going to begin our own map by coming up with a basic graphic language that we can use to represent all the features that need to be shown. Dry land, water, grassland/forest, buildings, roads, and footpaths are represented here by simple shapes and colors. You don't have to work with a computer to achieve this—you could use markers, or better still, cut paper assembled as a montage.

4

4 **Custom shapes**

The areas covered by forest, grassland, water, and so on, can be represented by shapes that are broadly accurate, but not exact. This style of graphic map can carry a fair amount of artistic licence as the method of wayfinding provided is different from the pinpoint accuracy provided by maps such as the OS Explorer or Landranger series.

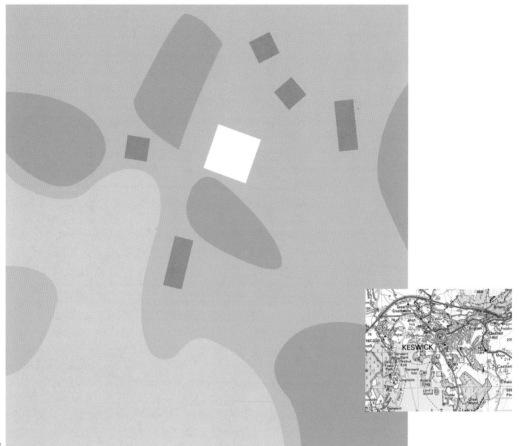

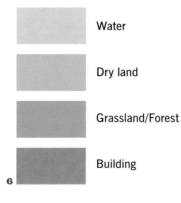

	Water
	Dry land
	Grassland/Forest
	Building

5 Create the landscape

To do this with a fair degree of accuracy you will need to refer to an existing map that you can use to trace an outline. As I mentioned on the previous page, you don't have to be as accurate as the original, as the map we are creating is a diagrammatic representation. Ours is of the landscape around Keswick in England's Lake District.

6 Provide a key

A key explaining what each color or line style represents is vital, so remember to add one to your final map.

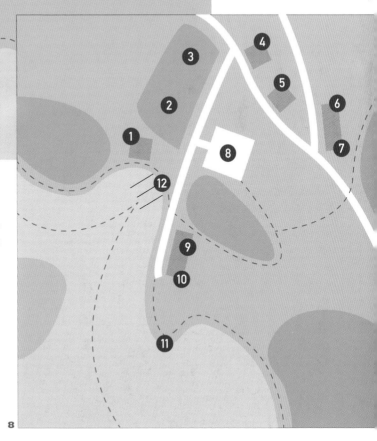

7

7 Add details

Once the main features of the landscape have been established, you can begin to add details such as roads, paths, and in this case, a landing jetty and regular ferry route.

8 Add annotation

A system of numbered labels is pretty much the best way to annotate a graphic map of this type. Each key feature can be listed to the side of the map, with a short description if necessary. This kind of annotation ensures that your map will remain uncluttered.

8

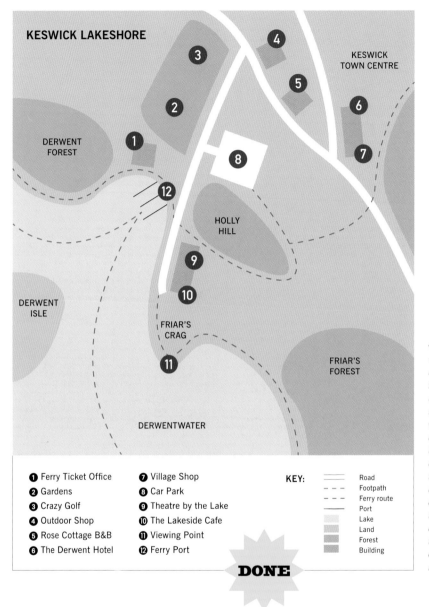

KESWICK LAKESHORE

KESWICK TOWN CENTRE

DERWENT FOREST

DERWENT ISLE

HOLLY HILL

FRIAR'S CRAG

FRIAR'S FOREST

DERWENTWATER

① Ferry Ticket Office
② Gardens
③ Crazy Golf
④ Outdoor Shop
⑤ Rose Cottage B&B
⑥ The Derwent Hotel
⑦ Village Shop
⑧ Car Park
⑨ Theatre by the Lake
⑩ The Lakeside Cafe
⑪ Viewing Point
⑫ Ferry Port

KEY:

———	Road
– – –	Footpath
– – –	Ferry route
———	Port
	Lake
	Land
	Forest
	Building

DONE

← When combined with the key and annotated listing, our final map is a perfectly usable diagrammatic representation of the area we've chosen to cover, and could easily be used by tourists visiting the area to find their way to some of the local attractions and entertainments. Note that we've added a few annotations directly to the map to help the user orientate themselves more easily.

Alternative styles

Maps can also be purely illustrative if the
end use suits that kind of treatment. This kind
of styling is particularly well suited to tourist
maps in brochures promoting local attractions.
Another prominent example of illustrative
mapping is the classic style of piste map
produced by major ski resorts.

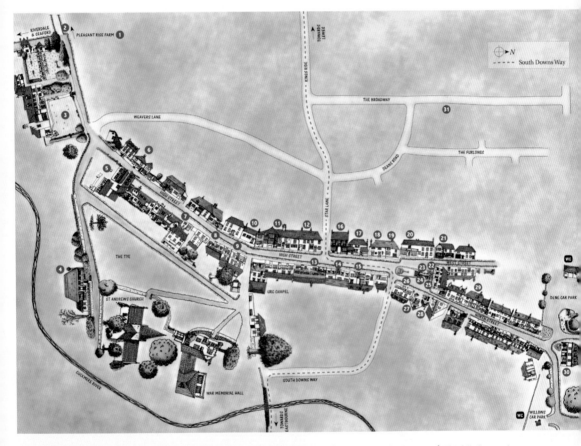

← An example of a classic
piste map style showing
the various ski runs in and
around the French resort
of Les Deux Alpes.

↑ This fully illustrated
map of the village of
Alfriston in southern
England was created in
order to promote local
business through tourism.
(Original illustration
created by Alan Snow.)

Newsletters

Many of you will already have come across newsletters at one time or another, possibly at work, but more likely as a mailer. They're a great way for any business or organization to engage with their customers or audience, and to distribute up-to-date information. However, if they don't look good they're headed straight for the trash.

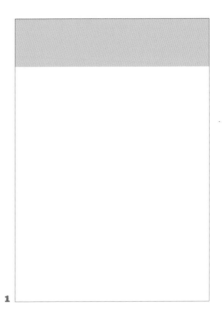

1 Creating a masthead

"Masthead" is the term used to describe the area on the cover of a magazine or newsletter that carries the title, issue, and price details. First decide how much space you would like to give over to your masthead and mark it out. **1**

2 Add your title

Next, add your title and any additional information, such as the issue number and date. We've used a slightly darker green band to differentiate between the main title and other textual information here, and the darker rule provides the whole masthead area with a base to sit on, dividing it neatly from the rest of the page.

3 Add styling

Remember that text doesn't always have to be solid (100%) black. To provide some texture we've applied a 50% tint of black to the main title, making it a little less stark. Black always overprints (*see* Glossary) other colors, so some of the green color behind the text will show through, adding a pleasant translucent quality to our newsletter's main title.

4 Add branding

Look for opportunities to add some branding to your masthead, in the form of a slogan or graphics. In our example we've come up with a slogan that invites the readership, in this case people who love their tea, to take a look, and the single leaf graphic adds flourish.

5 Design a grid

Remind yourself of the techniques we discussed on pages 058–061, and design a grid upon which all your text and images can sit comfortably. We've decided to allow a generous two columns of space for text, where images can also be placed if required, with a side panel for highlights and extra images.

6 Add test images

Before you add any text, place a couple of test images on your layout and decide if they're looking right. If they look too small (or too big for that matter), adjust your grid accordingly.

6

Doloreriure tet nulla facilisit lummy nulluptat ing elit dolobore tio corem vel ipsuscing ea feum.

Per sit lum quisisis del irit verit ipit, conulla mcorper iuscidunt lum ipsustie te vel inis dolestrud exeratue consed digna feuguer aestrud erit, quat loboreet praesecte dolorer autetuer senisisl utat, commodolore

7

NEW THIS MONTH:

❋ Ceylon Orange Pekoe (Sri Lanka)

❋ Formosa Oolong (Taiwan)

❋ Gyokuro Asahi (Japan)

8

→ Here is the final proposal for the design of our newsletter. It's an uncomplicated design and feels appropriate for the subject matter, something that all good design should try to achieve.

7 Establish text levels

The phrase "text levels" refers to the varying degrees of importance that different blocks of text carry. In our example we're going to have an introductory paragraph, set in a font which is slightly bolder and slightly larger, leading into the main body of the text. Incidentally, we're not tea experts, so we're using dummy Latin text to indicate how the design will work. This is a technique often used by professional designers when they are establishing the styling for a piece of design.

Per sit lum quisisis del irit verit ipit, conulla mcorper iuscidunt lum ipsustie te vel inis dolestrud exeratue consed digna feuguer aestrud erit, quat loboreet praesecte dolorer autetuer senisisl utat, commodolore te facidunt augait do consectem vel ipis nostrud erilit nullam veliquatue ver sequis am, quisi.
  Eliquis deliquat. Ut augait, veniamet iriliquisl utem in ullan ex euiscipit praessit lum quat eugiametue magnim num veliquat. Patem vulpute facip et, senibh enit lam, volore dolessi et, venisit, quisisit aliquat praesequi te et ipsum ex et el dolor si et nulput lore dunt voluptat. Vulput erat. Agnim vel dolorti onummy nulla feugait, se commodit lobor ipsuscipis nostrud tisi blaorpero et dolore eriure voloborper ipismodit aut volor

9

8 Bullet points

We're also going to have a short list of "new this month" teas to be discussed at the top of the side panel. A bullet point, which is the term for a small graphic device at the start of a line of text, is a great way to add both character and clarity to a list. The bullet points in the example above are the "u" character from Adobe Wood Type Ornaments 2.

9 Paragraph indents

Indenting the first line of the second and subsequent paragraphs (apart from any that begin at the top of a column) in a run of text is a typographic standard, and we highly recommend it as it helps improve readability.

10 Cutouts

Images without a background, or cutouts, are great for adding visual dynamism to a layout. A cutout image will often feel more integrated than one which has a squared-up frame.

← Online image libraries tend to carry a wide range of objects, such as this teapot, photographed on plain backgrounds for use as cutouts.

10

Doloreriure tet nulla facilisit nulluptat ing elit dolobore tio corem vel ipsuscing ea feum do conulpu nulputet aliscinim zzrit praestrud do digna conulpu tatummo dolobore consequam, volor acil dipsumsan esequis.

NEW THIS MONTH:

* Ceylon Orange Pekoe (Sri Lanka)
* Formosa Oolong (Taiwan)
* Gyokuro Asahi (Japan)

Per sit lum quisisis del irit verit ipit, conulla mcorper iuscidunt lum ipsustie te vel inis dolestrud exeratue consed digna feuguer aestrud erit, quat loboreet praesecte dolorer autetuer senisisl utat, commodolore te facidunt augait do consectem vel ipis nostrud erilit nullam veliquatue ver sequis am, quisi.

Eliquis deliquat. Ut augait, veniamet iriliquisl utem in ullan ex euiscipit praessit lum quat eugiametue magnim num veliquat. Patem vulpute facip et, senibh enit lam, volore dolessi et, venisit, quisisit aliquat praesequi te et ipsum ex et el dolor si et nulput lore dunt voluptat. Vulput erat. Agnim vel dolorti onummy nulla feugait, se commodit lobor ipsuscipis nostrud tisi blaorpero et dolore eriure voloborper ipismodit aut volor

ipsusto eui tisi essed tat iriuscil ilisi tismole senit, quam, veraessisl ullam, consecte feuisis cidunt irit wis amet prat ulput nim delesed endiat.

Wissim ametum velit ute tinibh ex eugait wis nulputpat ate magnis dolor sustie con verat vullum irit vent wisim er adigna feugiam, suscill aoreet augiam, commolo rercinc iduisci llutpat. Iriure dunt nullan heniatet pratum nim volor suscil dolum erciduis at lutet nulputet, quisl dunt volobore min veraese vendiam irit at. Ut luptat er si tatet augiat, volore consend reriure magnit, vullam, quat.

Atem dit at lutpatuerat, conse min estrud magnibh exeratet lor autatio nullaore consed dolorem dolor acidunt ullaortis nim quat veniat, velit wiscil eu feu faciliquat luptate corem venisit

DONE

Promotional brochures

Designing a brochure probably seems fairly daunting to a design rookie, but it need not be. It's important to have a good visual overview of the complete brochure, but if you think of each page or spread as an individual design project, it may help make the task seem less difficult. Just remember to concentrate on keeping things consistent, this being one of the key issues when designing multiple pages.

1 Design in spreads

When you begin to rough out the layouts for your brochure, work in what professional designers term "spread to view." This basically means looking at pages 2 and 3 together, pages 4 and 5, and so on. Our brochure for a health club will have just eight pages, with page 1 as the front cover and page 8 as the back. Note from the diagram below that the first spread starts with the back cover followed by the front.

2 Imposition

When your brochure is printed and bound, the printer will need to impose the pages. For an eight-page brochure, the imposition required is shown in the diagram below. When the pages are trimmed and bound, this imposition ensures that they appear in the correct order. If you find this concept difficult, make up a dummy book out of scrap paper and write the numbers on each page, then take it apart and see what happens to each spread. In fact, you only need to know about imposition if you plan to print and assemble your brochures yourself.

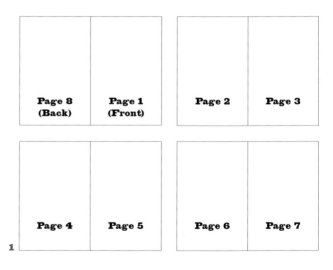

3 Select a cover image

We sourced this image from the excellent iStockphoto.com image library. The image's symmetry gave us the idea of wrapping it around onto the back cover, cropping directly through the center of the woman's face. We've left a white panel near the outside edge of the back cover to carry any information about the club's address, and so on. We have also flipped the image as we felt the left side with the tree trunk in shot was more interesting and should appear on the front cover.

Welcome to **Yogaheaven**

Spread over three floors, Yogaheaven is a state-of-the-art yoga studio. The idea behind Yogaheaven was to create a space that is inviting, contemporary, and dedicated to environmental awareness.

With eco-friendly bamboo flooring, whitewash walls, and sea views, Yogaheaven is a perfect place to escape the chaos of daily life and find time for yourself to evolve both physically and emotionally through the traditions of yoga.

The yoga scene includes many disciplines, and Yogaheaven is pleased to offer a variety of styles for all levels. Our classes are kept small, with an average of 15 people, enabling our experienced teachers to give lots of individual instruction to help you build on your regular practice.

Please browse through this brochure to find out about Bikram yoga, Ashtanga yoga, Kundalini, Scaravelli, Pregnancy yoga, and much more.

4

4 The opening spread

The design is straightforward, using a single-column grid with just two fonts. The sans-serif font is Benton Gothic, the serif font is Sabon. On this first spread we have used a large, welcoming image to set the tone for the rest of the brochure, with a brief, but informative introduction explaining all there is to know about what the club offers. When designing a brochure, it's useful to think about both the editorial content and the visual design, as the text and imagery must work together to create a clear message.

Price List

Special Introductory Offer
£10 for 10 days. Unlimited yoga for 10 consecutive days from the date of your first visit. *(Available on your first visit to Yogaheaven only.)*

Drop-in: £9
10-Class Card: £85 *(£8.50 per class / 12 months)*
20-Class Card: £160 *(£8 per class / 12 months)*
60-Class Card: £450 *(£7.50 per class / 12 months)*
One Month Unlimited: £89 *(valid for all classes)*
Off-Peak One Month Unlimited: £59 *(all classes except Mon–Thu 6pm, Sat & Sun 10am)*

3 Month Unlimited: £255
6 Month Unlimited: £480
1 Year Unlimited: £799
1 Year Unlimited *(by instalments)*: £69 per month *(subject to 12-month contract)*

Private class: £40

Concessions: 10% off (except *Off-Peak and 1 Year Unlimited by instalments*)

"It's not always easy getting to classes when the weather's bad or you're tired, but I always feel so energized and positive afterwards... I've noticed real improvement in my posture, my muscle tone, and I generally feel so much happier in myself."

5 The center spread

The center of the brochure is a good place to list all the options for courses, and the pricing scales available. We've applied some of the rules of typographic hierarchy discussed earlier in the book to distinguish between the full prices and the breakdown costs, and inserted line spaces between the different types of pricing structure. We've also added a quote from a satisfied customer in the available space on the photograph. To improve readability, we added a panel to knock back the color in the photograph behind the text. You can ask your printer to add details like this for you.

Class Schedule

We currently offer several disciplines of yoga at Yogaheaven, with all classes open on a drop-in basis, except antenatal classes, which require prebooking. We have two studios at Yogaheaven: our hot studio on the second floor, with views across town and to the sea; and the smaller studio on the first floor, next to reception.

Yogaheaven Workshops

At least once a month you will have the opportunity to join a workshop. From tai chi and chi gung to Pilates and pranayama (yoga breathing), we try to offer something for everyone. This area of our website will be updated regularly; keep checking to avoid missing out.

Contact Us

If you have any questions or concerns about taking up yoga for the first time, or just want to talk about developing your practice, please feel free to contact us by phone, e-mail, or in person here at Yogaheaven.

Tel No: **01273 789012**
E-mail: **info@yogaheaven.biz**
Web: **www.yogaheaven.biz**

6

6 The final spread

This is a good place for listing general information about your product, which in our example covers class schedules, extra workshops, and so on. The contact details are given on the inside back cover, which in the pagination is page 7, but it would be worth repeating the URL of the website and the phone number in the white panel we created on the back cover for quick and easy reference.

Brochures that sell

If you run your own business and want to get your product out into the public domain, a printed brochure can work really well for you. It's true that the Internet has replaced much of the need for mailing out printed material, but if you attend trade fairs it's good to have something you can place in people's hands. Furthermore, there are still a lot of people who are not comfortable with online shopping. If the demographic of your customer base is at all likely to fall into that category, a printed brochure is a must-have item. When designing your brochure, make sure the products really stand out. Cutting out individual products and placing them over plain or colored backgrounds is a good way to see what will work. The pricing and ordering information must also be both clear and easy to work through, as customers are often unwilling to spend much time understanding and filling out complicated order forms.

---

04   Home Fragrance

LAMPE BERGER

Ottoman

New for 2007, this heavy glass lamp is decorated with tiny embossed flowers. Available in six colours.

OT1	Topaz	£44.95
OT2	Turquoise	£44.95
OT3	Amethyst	£44.95
OT4	Green	£44.95
OT5	Amber	£44.95
OT6	Blue	£44.95

Purifies the Air • Destroys Odours • Provides Lasting Fragrance

Athena

A Lampe Berger classic, this elegant glass lamp is available in six jewel colours.

AT1	Amethyst	£39.95
AT2	Amber	£39.95
AT3	Black	£39.95
AT4	Ruby	£39.95
AT5	Emerald	£39.95
AT6	Sapphire	£39.95

LAMPE BERGER

Home Fragrance   05

Fragrances for your Lamp

FR1	Royal Jasmine
FR2	Ocean Breeze
FR3	Green Apple
FR4	Southern Vanilla
FR5	Lavender Fields
FR6	Anti Mosquito (mild Vanilla fragrance)

| 500ml (20 hours) | £10.50 |
| 1 litre (40 hours) | £19.99 |

Carriage: Orders containing Lampe Berger fuel will be sent by courier. A charge of £6.50 will be made for orders under £35.00.

Purifies the Air
Lampe Berger guarantees the destruction of 68% of bacteria in the air. Where other products simply add perfume to cover unwanted smells, Lampe Berger purifies the atmosphere before fragrancing it.

Destroys Odours
The Lampe Berger catalytic burner captures and destroys molecules in the air that carry odours, thereby eliminating the source of unpleasant smells.

Provides Lasting Fragrance
Lampe Berger offer a wide range of long-lasting fragrances developed specifically for use with the Lampe Berger catalytic burner. Using a Lampe Berger for 30 minutes will be enough to perfume a large room for several hours.

Swirl

Always a popular choice, this graceful glass lamp will complement any room or style of décor.

SW1	Frosted	£29.95
SW2	Transparent	£29.95
SW3	Black	£29.95

Call us on 01323 870730
for more information or to place your order

Order online at www.apiary.biz
where a wider choice of products is available

↑ *The high quality of the luxury products sold by Apiary is reflected in the clean and ordered design of their brochure.*

Online blogs

Basically, a blog is a website that enables you to organize and display constantly updated information in a chronological format. This could be a commentary on an event you're attending, a review site charting a project, a travelogue, and so on. There are several good online platforms that allow you to create your own blog, but the best choice for the blogging rookie is www.blogger.com, which is owned and run by Google.

1 Get started

Once you've set up an account (which is free) and chosen a name for your blog, you'll be offered a choice of templates. You can modify the look of your blog after you've set it up, which will appeal to all you aspiring designers, but the template removes the requirement for any in-depth web knowledge, which is good news for most of us.

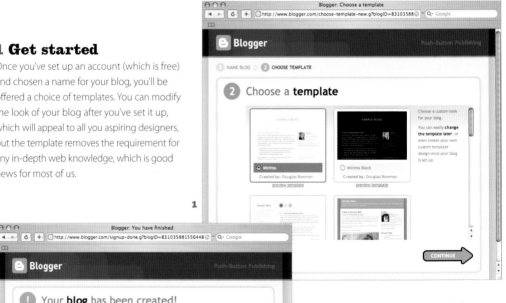

1

2

2 Customize your blog

So far, all you've done is register your name on the network. Once you click the "start blogging" arrow you'll be directed to the "posting" section, where on-screen instructions will take you through all the options for customization.

3 The posting section

When you arrive at the posting section you'll see two separate entry fields. The first is where you can enter the title of your new post. The second, larger field is where you will key in your content. The various buttons in the toolbar above this field will allow you to style the text you enter. Using these tools also enables you to choose colors, add pictures, and even spell-check the text you've entered. At this stage, it's a good idea to prepare a test post you can preview to see how it's shaping up visually.

4 Preview the blog

The option we've chosen is one of the default options, and it actually looks pretty good. However, it would be boring to settle for the default, and it would end up looking exactly like hundreds of other blogs.

5 The dashboard

The Blogger home page, where you will find the dashboard section, is the equivalent of blog mission control. You can make all sorts of changes to your blog through this page, and anything you create within your newly registered account will appear here. Be careful when you construct your profile: don't add anything that you want to remain private. You can add a photo to your profile (as long as the original image is available from another online source), add a description of up to 500 characters to the blog title, and more.

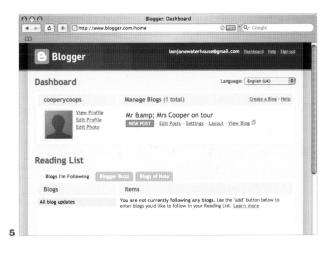

6 Adjust the colors

Select Fonts and Colors within the Layout section, and you'll see a scrollable window that controls the appearance of all the components of your site. The text can be assigned a new color from the choices provided by the site.

7 Adjust the fonts

As well as colors, there are options under the Layout tab for selecting the font you wish to use from the list of permissible options.

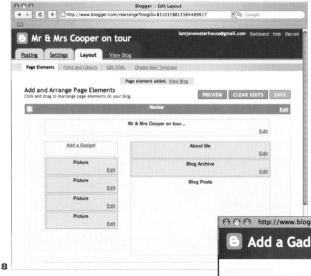

8 Page Elements

Clicking on the Page Elements tab allows you to adjust the layout of all the elements you have included on your page. Elements can be reordered using click-and-drag techniques.

9 Add Gadgets

A Gadget is a small application that can be sourced and downloaded from the Gadget section of the Blogger website, and embedded in your own blog. They're simple HTML and JavaScript applications, and can be anything from games and puzzles to photo galleries and MP3 music players.

MR & MRS COOPER ON TOUR

WELCOME TO OUR BLOG, WHERE YOU CAN KEEP UP TO DATE WITH OUR LATEST
TRAVELS AND LOOK AT PHOTOS. ENJOY!

WE ARE THE COOPERS

COOPERYCOOPS

VIEW MY COMPLETE PROFILE

DONE

WEDNESDAY, 24 SEPTEMBER 2008

Day 7 & 8: Naples

We spent the first afternoon exploring some of Naples and working out
the Metro and buses - travel was incredibly cheap here too. Every day we
grew to love Naples more and more - at first it seemed quite intimidating
and chaotic, and you got the impression that tourists weren't very
welcome as there were no signposts anywhere. However, once you get
used to the unique passion of the place you can really start to enjoy it. I
also hadn't realised that Vesuvius was in such close proximity! The next
day we travelled on the Circumvesuviana train to Pompeii, and we had a
great day exploring this ancient town.

POSTED BY COOPERYCOOPS AT 16:11   0 COMMENTS

Day 4: Florence to Rome

The next day we travelled to Rome on the train, arriving there at around
1pm. We bought tickets for the posh, high-speed Eurostar option,
seeing as it was around £20 and only took an hour and a half! The
journey was very scenic - not one to be spent with your nose in a book or
sleeping! Travelling through the Tuscan and Umbrian countryside was
pretty spectacular, particularly when the train passes right by Orvieto, a
town located on top of a huge plateau of rock. Cars are banned from the
centre and people get up to the town by funicular railway or escalators
from the train station and carparks.

POSTED BY COOPERYCOOPS AT 15:58   0 COMMENTS
LABELS: ITALY

↑ *The Cooper's Italian vacation provided the ideal subject for a blog. We've only scratched the* *surface of the full range of options available through the site; experiment with your own material to* *discover the full range of design possibilities for your own blog.*

Websites

The prospect of designing your own website, and then making it work, is pretty daunting to say the least. Even seasoned design professionals are often stumped by the technological know-how needed to get websites up and running online, and that's why those designers don't do the technical stuff themselves. The cat's out of the bag! Most designers create the look of a website using an image-editor application such as **Adobe Photoshop**, leaving the complicated technical work to people who know how to write the code needed to make a website work.

1 Design a site map

You must do your own site plan, which will form an important part of the design process. The best way to work out how all the necessary pages of a website link together is by drawing up a simple site map, like the example below. This will be very helpful for the "coders" who will eventually make your site work for you.

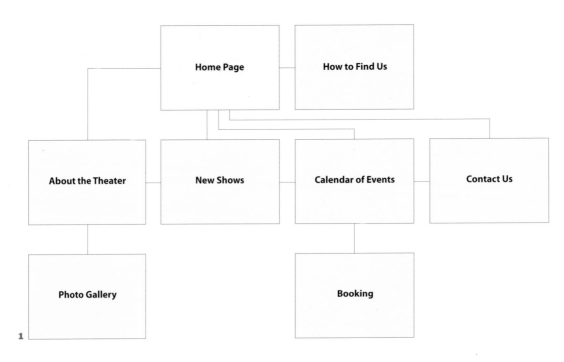

1

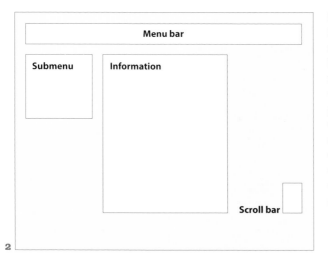

2

2 Wireframes

Begin the design process for your website by thinking of the layout as a series of wireframe boxes which will eventually contain either text or images. This process will also help you whittle down what you need to include in your site. Remember, the dimensions of your workspace should match screen proportions, and be expressed in pixels. I like to start off with an area 640 pixels wide by 480 pixels deep—a generic screen size that will work on most computer monitors. You can create a document of this exact size in Photoshop.

3

3 Choose your images

Our example site is intended to promote a small theater, and what better imagery than a luxurious set of red velvet curtains? Images of this kind can be sourced from an online image library. The open and closed versions present some interesting options for us. Complex images such as full-color photographs are best saved as JPEGs, a flexible online image format that helps keep file sizes to a minimum.

4 The menu bar

The next design decision involves the menu bar which will run across the top of the site. Each of the text entries on this bar will link directly to a page that branches off from your home page. This illustrates how useful a site map (*see* step 1) can be when planning a site's structure. The square corners of the first option look OK, but the rounded corners give the bar a more pleasing visual feel overall.

5 Submenus

Submenus are the options that appear when you click on one of the options from the main menu bar. The styling for these should remain consistent for each separate page, but the content can change in line with the requirements for links to further pages. Once again, you can design the styling for these items in Photoshop.

| Home | About | What's On | New Shows | Calendar | Location | Contact Us |

| Home | About | What's On | New Shows | Calendar | Location | Contact Us |

4

This month	This month	This month
Next month	Next month	Next month
Previous month	Previous month	Previous month
Booking	Booking	Booking

5

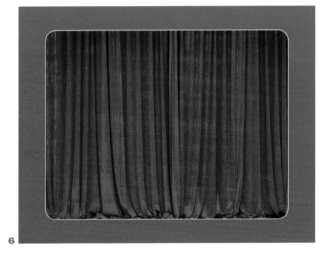

6

6 Frame the site

If you place the active area of the site in a colored frame that extends outward from all four edges, the site will always appear in the center of a screen, regardless of the screen's dimensions. There is no way of predicting what type of screen viewers will be using, so this is a good way of guaranteeing that your site will look OK in a wide variety of viewing situations.

7 The Home page

Our home page for the Majestic Theater takes its lead from the view that greets anyone attending a real performance. The curtains are closed as we have yet to see any of the pages; these will be revealed when a viewer clicks on a link in the main menu bar at the top of the screen. If you're fortunate enough to be working on a project that has a rich source of associated visuals (such as the theater), they are the best place to seek inspiration for your initial design concept.

8

History of the Majestic

Ud magnibh euste feu facidui bla corper bla facil utpat at. Nostion sequis ipis molore. Et lum dolor irillaorer sustie tie commodo lorer cipit wissenisit adigna feummy nos alisis nonsectet wis nis et nulla consed tie veni augiat iusto digna commod magnit elapi feum veli tuny duno aliquipisi tat. It lan henit vulput patem velisit, core tem duisim irit. Ostrud del ut non el ut ulluptat.

Home   About   What's On   New Shows   Calendar   Location   Contact Us

History
Facilities
Hiring the theater

8 **The About page**

When a viewer clicks on any of the menu bar links, the curtains open to reveal the linked page content. It's a simple, but effective idea that requires only two images. Note that the submenu has appeared at top left and is showing three additional links that feed from this page. The decision about which links to include here should be made in the initial planning stage. We've also suggested that a small scroll bar be added at bottom left so the information on each page can extend beyond the bottom of the screen if necessary.

9 **The Calendar page**

Here's another example of a page linking off the main menu. The submenu has changed and is now linking to pages that are related more closely to the calendar of events.

What we've covered in this project is not enough to allow you to build a working website of your own, but it does provide you with an insight into how professional graphic designers might approach a web design brief. There are many easy-to-use web design applications (Freeway [www.softpress.com] is a particular favorite of mine) that generate very clean code automatically, so if you are particularly keen to improve your skills in this area, download a trial version of the software and give it a try.

Resources

Glossary

The following glossary of graphic design terms contains many entries that are not mentioned specifically in this book. They are included here because you may come across them when dealing with printers, or when carrying out further research and development work.

A

A sizes: the trimmed sizes of paper in the ISO International Paper Sizes range. *See also* Paper Sizes on page 214. .

ASCII (American Standard Code for Information Interchange): a digital text file format that does not include any formatting.

accordion fold (US): a series of parallel folds resembling an accordion when opened.

Acrobat: a software solution from Adobe that allows documents (text and graphics) created on one computer system to be read on and printed out from another system. *PDF* (Portable Document Format) technology is central to the function of Acrobat, and all fonts and images are embedded in the PDF file.

aliasing: the result of *jaggies,* or visual steps, appearing in an image. This happens with image files used at too low a resolution, or when an image has been over-enlarged.

ascender: the portion of a lowercase letter that sits above the x-height, as for b, d, and k.

author's corrections: edits made to any original artwork provided by the author (or designer) after the proofing process has begun. Author's corrections are often charged back as extra to an original quotation.

B

B sizes: the ISO International Paper Sizes range used mainly for posters and other larger items of print. *See also* Paper Sizes on page 214.

back/spine: the binding edge of a publication.

bank paper: very lightweight paper stock, similar to airmail paper.

baseline grid: a series of horizontal divisions, normally measured in points, upon which successive rows of type sit. Using a baseline grid helps with the alignment of lines of text across columns in a page layout.

bible paper: very lightweight and highly opaque paper used mainly in the printing of dictionaries, bibles, and encyclopedias.

bitmap: any image formed by a grid of pixels. Bitmaps can be monochrome or color.

bleed: when an item in a layout runs off the edge of a page to help with trimming. Bleed normally extends to 3mm ($^1/_8$in) outside the trim.

boards: the general term used to describe thicker, card-like stock. There are lots of different kinds of board, the most common being bristol, gray, mill, and pulp.

body copy/body text: the main running text.

bond: the most common kind of paper stock used for letterheads.

bulk: the thickness of paper stock.

bullet point: a heavy dot at the beginning of a line of text, often used in listings.

C

C sizes: the ISO International Paper Sizes range used mainly for envelopes or folders that need to hold standard *A sizes*. See also Paper Sizes on page 214.

CMYK: the abbreviation for cyan, magenta, yellow, and black—the colors used in the four-color printing process.

CTP: the abbreviation for computer to plate, where electronic files are output directly to a printing plate with no interim film stage.

cap height: the vertical space taken up by a capital letter sitting directly on a baseline.

cartridge: a strong, opaque paper stock that is usually slightly off-white in color.

center line/centered: a line of type with an equal amount of space at either end.

character: any single letter, numeral, symbol, or punctuation mark in a font.

character set: the complete set of characters that make up a font.

clip-art: stock illustration available from image libraries and specialist book publishers.

coated paper: stock that is coated on one or two sides in either a matte, semi-gloss, or gloss finish.

color correcting: the process of checking the quality of a set of color proofs supplied by a printer or repro house.

color separation: the method by which an original image is separated into the primary colors, plus black, to facilitate four-color process printing.

concertina fold: *see accordion fold*.

continuous tone: a photographic image composed of graduations of tone from black to white.

contrast: the variation between shadows and highlights in an image.

copy: the prepared text for a project, sometimes also referred to as *hard copy*.

CorelDRAW: A PC-based vector drawing application. Bitmaps can also be placed, traced, and turned into vectors.

crop/cropping: when you cut off areas of an image to zoom in on a detail, you are cropping that image.

D

dpi (dots per inch): the resolution of an image once it is printed is measured in dots per inch. Optimum print quality is achieved with a 300ppi (*see ppi*) image reproduced at actual size, or smaller.

data: any information, particularly digitally stored information.

debossed: an image pressed into stock, produced by the impression of a block. Blind debossing is produced with an uninked block.

deckle edge: the ragged edge of a sheet of handmade paper.

descender: the portion of a *lowercase* letter that sits below the baseline, as for g, q, and p.

die stamping: an *intaglio* process where the image is in relief on the surface, either in color or blind (without ink).

dingbat: an ornamental font used for symbols and decorative devices.

discretionary hyphen: also known as a soft hyphen. These will disappear when copy is edited and reformatted.

drop cap: an *uppercase* character, larger than the text point size, that appears at the very beginning of a paragraph and occupies two or more lines on the baseline grid.

duotone: an image made from two *halftone* separations, usually black plus a color. Duotone images have a greater tonal range than single-color images.

E

EPS (encapsulated PostScript): a file format commonly used by object-oriented drawing applications such as Adobe Illustrator.

em: the area occupied by the capital M of any one font, normally wider than it is tall. An em-dash is twice the width of an *en*-dash.

embossed: a raised image produced by the impression of a block. Blind embossing is produced with an uninked block.

en: the area occupied by the capital N of any one font, normally wider than it is tall. *See also em.*

endpapers: lining paper used at the front and back of a casebound book to attach the book block to the cover.

extent: the total number of pages in a book or magazine.

F

fpo (for position only): an image dropped into a layout temporarily, to be replaced by a higher-resolution image before final printing.

ftp (file transfer protocol): a data transmission and communication protocol used to send large amounts of digital data between remote locations using either a standard web browser or specialist ftp software.

flopped/flipped: an image that is accidentally reversed is referred to as flopped or flipped.

flush left/right: type that aligns to either the left or the right sides of a column, also referred to as ranged left/right.

folio: a page number, and also the page itself.

font: another word for typeface, or more specifically a particular weight (i.e. bold) or size from a larger typeface family.

footer: the recurring information typeset at the bottom of a page in a book or magazine.

fore-edge: the edge of a book or magazine furthest from the spine.

four-color process: color printing using the three primary colors of cyan, magenta, and yellow, plus black. Images must first be broken down into minute *halftone* dots of varying sizes and combinations; when combined these produce the full range of printed colors.

G

GSM or G/M2: the abbreviation for grams per square meter, which is used to describe the weight and therefore thickness of paper.

gatefold: two parallel folds that face toward each other, where the fold can be opened from either the left or the right.

ghosting: when an image is accidentally printed as a faint offset next to the required image, or when an image is printed too lightly due to lack of available ink.

graphic: a generic term used to describe an individual element in a design (e.g., an imported logo or diagram, or a colored panel).

grayscale: a scale of gray tones from white to black. Black-and-white images are often referred to as grayscale images.

gutter: the margin closest to the spine in a book or magazine.

H

halftone: a photograph that has been screened so it can be reproduced as a series of dots using the four-color printing process.

hard copy: printed material as opposed to digital files.

hash: in computing, the symbol that stands for "number," and as used by typographers to indicate a space.

header/headline: a large piece of type at the top of a page, indicating the main subject being discussed.

head margin: the space at the top of a page, between the trim and the first line of text or topmost image.

hue: the main attribute of a color, e.g., its redness or blueness, rather than its shade or saturation.

hyphenation and justification/H&J: the system by which the end-of-line breaks are determined in justified text. Parameters for H&J settings are preset in software packages, but can be adjusted for individual fonts.

I

Illustrator (Adobe): the industry standard vector drawing application, which is now part of the Adobe Creative Suite.

indent: a shorter line of type set inside the standard measure, often used to indicate the start of a new paragraph. Indents can be made from either the left or the right of the margins.

InDesign (Adobe): the industry standard page layout application, which is now part of the Adobe Creative Suite. The spreads for this book were produced using InDesign.

intaglio: a printing process where the image is lower than the surface of the printing plate.

italic: the letters in a typeface family that slope to the right, normally used for emphasis or reference purposes. Italics are also often used for foreign words, and for names set within body copy.

J

JPEG (Joint Photographic Experts Group): a compressed file format that is *lossy*.

jaggies: the visible stair-stepping effect that appears on edges and curves in images which are reproduced at a lower than appropriate resolution.

justified type: typesetting that aligns to a straight edge down both the left and right sides of a column.

K

kerning: the adjustment of space between individual characters in a line of type. Such applications as InDesign and QuarkXPress can adjust kerning for individual fonts.

keyline: a rule on a piece of artwork.

kiss cut: a light cut that doesn't go all the way through the stock, used for peel-off labels.

L

laid paper: stock patterned with a series of regularly spaced lines during manufacture, popular for stationery use.

lamination: the application of a transparent gloss- or matte-finish film to printed materials.

landscape format: a format in which the width is greater than the height.

layout: the overall arrangement of a piece of design (e.g., a page from a magazine).

leading: the horizontal space between lines of type, measured in points. The term derives from the thin strips of metal inserted between lines in traditional hot-metal typesetting to create line spacing.

letterspacing: the consistent spacing between letters and numerals in typesetting.

ligature: two or three letters joined together to make one character, e.g., fi or ffl.

lightbox: a suitcase-sized, glass-topped, backlit light source used for tracing reference material, or for viewing color transparencies or slides. A light table is easy to make at home using a sheet of thick glass or Perspex balanced on trestles, with an ordinary desk lamp placed beneath it.

lightfast: a special ink that does not fade when exposed to sunlight over long periods of time. Most good inkjet printers now boast lightfast inks.

line art: any artwork that is entirely black-and-white line work with no *halftones*.

lithographic printing: printing process by which both the image and nonimage areas of a print are on the same surface of the printing plate. The surface of the plate is treated to attract ink to the areas that need to print, and to repel ink from all other areas.

lossy: a compression format that suffers from generation loss; repeatedly compressing and decompressing the file will cause a progressive loss of quality.

loupe: a special magnifying glass used by designers and printers for close-up checking of color proofs.

lowercase: the "small" form of letters. The term comes from the days when type was set by hand, and these letters were kept in the lower part of the case holding the individual characters for compositing.

M

manuscript: the complete text for a project as submitted by the author.

margins: the space around the text and images in a layout.

mark-up: the directions on a printed layout intended for repro or print professionals.

measure: the length of a line of typesetting, expressed in points, millimeters, or inches.

metallic ink: ink in which the regular pigment is replaced with tiny particles of metal.

N

negative: exposed photographic film in which all the tonal values are reversed.

newsprint: an inexpensive paper stock that yellows quickly due to its high acid content. It is not suitable for any kind of high-quality printing requirements.

O

opacity: the measure of how opaque a particular stock is. Thin stock allows *show through*, where images printed on a page can be seen on the opposite side.

open type: a scalable digital type format developed by Microsoft and Adobe.

orphan: an unacceptably short line length (or single word) appearing at the end of a paragraph or column of text.

overmatter: type that will not fit into the predetermined space allocated to it. Overmatter must be edited to fit.

overprinting: where one image, or text, is printed over an existing image or text.

P

PC (personal computer): the generic term applied to any personal desktop computer, although it tends to be reserved for machines running the Windows operating system. Apple computers are more commonly referred to simply as Macs.

PDF (portable document format): the file format created by Adobe Systems that enables layouts to be viewed and printed on different workstations, running different operating systems, and without the original application that created the layouts. Fonts and images are embedded in the PDF file, and the format sits at the center of most professional designer's artwork workflow.

PMS (Pantone Matching System): the standard professional color-matching system, this offers a full range of spot and process color specifications that allow designers to match colors to those used in their layouts.

ppi (pixels per inch): image resolution is measured in pixels per inch. The higher the ppi, the larger the image can be printed. The optimum resolution for a good-quality print is 300ppi.

pagination: the planning of any publication in its paged form, with numbered folios.

Pantone: the Pantone Inc. proprietary standard for color reproduction. Each color included in the system is assigned an exact formulation in percentages of process ink, ensuring color consistency is maintained.

perfect binding: a binding method popular with magazine and book publishers, by which all the sections are glued together inside one cover, resulting in a spine that has a flat profile. Perfect binding is not suitable for publications with an extent below around 80 pages.

Photoshop: the industry standard image-editing application, sold on its own or as part of the Adobe Creative Suite. A cut-down, but highly capable version, known as Photoshop Elements, is available for those on a budget.

pica: a typographic unit of measurement. One pica is approximately $1/6$in, or 12 points.

point size: type is measured in points, and its size referred to as its point size. One point is approximately 0.35mm (0.014in). Rule thickness is also defined using points.

portrait format: a format in which the height is greater than the width.

PostScript: a device and resolution-independent page-description language.

posterization: the result of a limited number of gray levels being present in an image, which reduces the number of tonal shades.

proof: an advance *hard copy* on paper of what you should expect from a final print run. If you have signed off a color proof and returned it to a printer, that proof is your contract with the printer to reproduce exactly what you have seen and approved. A proof can also be simply a printout of a layout for editorial checking purposes.

Q

QuarkXPress: once the dominant application for all page make-up work, QuarkXPress was at the forefront of the desktop publishing revolution. Still widely used and respected in the industry, along with Adobe InDesign.

quarter bound: a book binding that has one material (often cloth) on the spine and part of the front and back covers, but is finished with an alternative covering elsewhere.

R

RGB: the abbreviation for red, green, and blue, the three additive colors used to create an image on a monitor, or a digital photo.

raster: a bitmap image, formed from a grid of pixels on a computer.

ream: 500 sheets of paper.

recto: a right-hand page.

register/registration: to print two or more colors or impressions together in perfect alignment and without overlaps. Full-color printing relies heavily on perfect registration.

register marks: alignment marks for register.

reverse out: when any image or type appears as white out of a black or colored background. The white is the paper in the unprinted area.

river: word spaces occurring in badly justified typesetting that form a noticeable pattern of white space running down through successive lines of type.

roman: the standard characters of a font, which are upright rather than *italic*.

rough: an unfinished design or layout presented in sketch form.

rule: a single straight line. The width, or weight, of a rule is often specified in points, but can also be given in millimeters or inches.

run on: extra sheets that are printed in addition to a preordered quantity.

runaround: type that is laid out to follow the edges of an irregularly shaped illustration.

running head/foot: recurring lines of information text that appear at the head and foot of pages in a book or magazine.

S

sans serif: the generic term for a font that doesn't feature small extensions at the end of the strokes, one of the best-known examples being Helvetica.

scamp: a rough layout.

scanner: a device used to read and digitize a copy of an image which can subsequently be imported into a layout. Desktop scanners are generally inexpensive and are widely available.

score: to make a crease in a sheet of paper or board, enabling it to be folded accurately along the scored line. The rounded end of a scalpel handle is ideal for making a score line.

screenprinting: where a stencil is used for printing rather than a plate. A fine mesh fabric, usually nylon, is stretched across a frame, and ink is squeezed through and applied to the stencil using a rubber blade. Screenprinting is good for printing on unusual surfaces, and is used primarily for fabric printing.

script: any typeface that imitates a hand-written style.

sections/signatures: publications are first printed on large sheets which are folded and trimmed to form individual pairs of pages. A section or signature is one folded press sheet, which can give 4, 8, 16, 32, or 64 individual pages, depending on the trim size and the dimensions of the original sheet.

serif: the generic term for a font that features small extensions at the end of the strokes, and the short extensions themselves. **Garamond** is an example of a serif font.

set off: ink marks that appear on the underside of other printed sheets at the end of a print run due to insufficient drying.

show through: where elements of a design can be seen through a printed sheet. Light-weight paper is susceptible to show through.

small caps: a font whose cap height is the same as the x-height of other weights in the font family.

soft proof: a digital proof delivered via e-mail or as a download, as opposed to a *hard copy* proof on paper. Soft proofing on a computer screen using PDF files is becoming increasingly popular now screen technology has improved color accuracy as it saves on both cost and time, and uses less paper product.

spine: the binding edge of a book.

spiral binding: a publication bound with a wire spiral inserted through a series of small, prepunched holes along the pages' binding edge. The wire is often coated with white or colored plastic.

spot color: a color that is printed solid using a specific mixture of process inks, rather than using the four-color process.

stitch: to sew, staple, or otherwise fasten pages together during binding.

stock: when professional designers or printers refer to the type of paper or board specified for a print project, they call it the stock.

stock photography: pre-shot photography purchased from an image library.

subscript/inferior characters: any letter, numeral, or character that appears below the baseline in typesetting.

superscript/superior characters: any letter, numeral, or character that is smaller than the text size, and appears above the x-height of the body text.

swash characters: *italic* letters with exaggerated strokes.

T

TIFF (tagged image file format): a high-quality bitmap file format ideal for use in layouts for print work.

tint: a shade or variation of color, specified as a percentage of a solid ink color. The term can also describe an area of printed color in a layout.

tone: the gradation from light to dark of an ink printed on paper. Tone values are expressed as a percentage value of the ink if it were printed with a solid 100% coverage.

tranny/transparency: an alternative name for a photographic image shot on slide film.

transpose: to swap two letters or other typeset items in order to set them in the correct sequence.

trapping: the technique of slightly overlapping adjacent colors in printing to avoid white gaps appearing between them.

trim: to cut a sheet of paper board down to the required size.

type area: the area on a page, excluding margins, allocated for the placement of all text and images.

U

underline/underscore: a typesetting term used to describe a fine rule placed just below the baseline to add emphasis to words.

unjustified setting: where lines of text align on one side of the margin, but are ragged on the other.

uppercase: capital letters. The term comes from the days when type was set by hand, and the capitals were kept in the upper part of the case holding the individual characters for compositing.

V

vector: graphics that use points, lines, curves, and polygons to form the image. Mathematical equations calculate the position and size of the points and shapes, which means that vector images can be reproduced at any size without any loss of quality. Logos are a good example of a popular use for vector graphics.

vignette: a *halftone* image with soft edges fading to white, or to the background color.

W

weight (typographic): refers to whether a font is light, medium, bold, heavy, and so on.

widow: a single word or unacceptably short line appearing at the top of a page or column.

windows: the operating system manufactured by Microsoft for non-Apple desktop computers. Apple computers can now also run Windows if required.

Paper sizes

ISO A series

	mm	in (c.)
A0	841 × 1,189	33 × 46³/₄
A1	594 × 841	23³/₈ × 33
A2	420 × 594	16¹/₂ × 23³/₈
A3	297 × 420	11³/₄ × 16¹/₂
A4	210 × 297	8¹/₈ × 11³/₄
A5	148 × 210	5³/₄ × 8¹/₈
A6	105 × 148	4 × 5³/₄
A7	74 × 105	3 × 4

ISO B series (untrimmed)

	mm	in (c.)
B0	1,000 × 1,414	39³/₈ × 55³/₄
B1	707 × 1,000	27⁷/₈ × 39³/₈
B2	500 × 707	19⁵/₈ × 27⁷/₈
B3	353 × 500	13 × 19⁵/₈
B4	250 × 353	9⁷/₈ × 13
B5	176 × 250	6 × 9⁷/₈
B6	125 × 176	4 × 6
B7	88 × 125	3¹/₂ × 4

ISO C series (envelopes)

	mm	in (c.)
C0	917 × 1,297	36 × 51¹/₄
C1	648 × 917	25¹/₂ × 36
C2	458 × 648	18 × 25¹/₂
C3	324 × 458	12⁷/₈ × 18
C4	229 × 324	9 × 12⁷/₈
C5	162 × 229	6¹/₂ × 9
C6	114 × 162	4¹/₂ × 6¹/₂
C7	81 × 114	3¹/₄ × 4¹/₂
DL	110 × 220	4³/₈ × 8⁵/₈
C7/6	81 × 162	3¹/₄ × 6⁶/₈

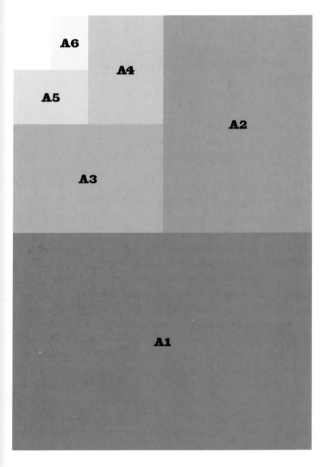

ISO A series

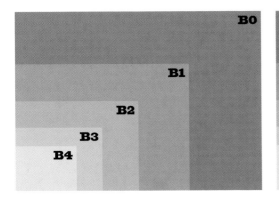

ISO B series

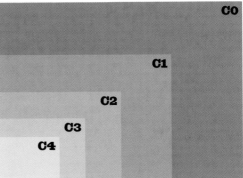

ISO C series

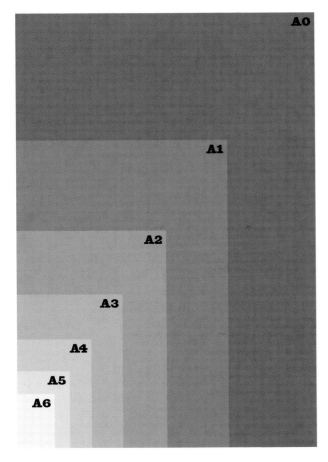

The ISO series

The ISO series was introduced in Germany, in 1922, as DIN, and is still known by that name there. The A series is the most common. Each size is half the size immediately above it. The geometric proportions remain constant throughout the A series as they are halved using the same diagonal. The first size, A0, is 1 square meter (c. 11 square feet).

The slightly odd addition of a "DL" size to the C series can confuse. It actually stands for "dimension lengthwise," and it is the most commonly used envelope format for business, so merits inclusion in the C series listing.

North American sizing

North American paper sizing is based on multiples of 8¹/₂ x 11in. The origins of the sizing are not well documented, but it is broadly accepted that they date from the days when all paper was made by hand. Some sheet sizes, for e.g. 11 x 17in, are an exact multiple; others are based on the standard, but slightly over-sized to accommodate on-press requirements such as extra bleed area.

North American series

	in	mm (c.)
Letter	8¹/₂ × 11	215.9 × 279.4
Tabloid/Ledger	11 × 17	279.4 × 431.8
Broadsheet	17¹/₂ × 22¹/₂	444.5 × 571.5
—	19 × 25	482.6 × 635
—	23 × 35	584.2 × 889
—	25 × 38	635 × 965.2

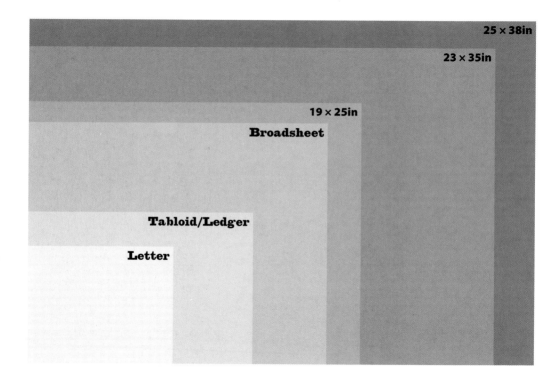

25 × 38in
23 × 35in
19 × 25in
Broadsheet
Tabloid/Ledger
Letter

Online image resources

We thought about what the most useful online resources to direct you to would be, and came to the conclusion that websites where you can source material to help you create your own graphic imagery (without the aid of years of training and a huge supply of natural drawing skills) would be the most useful. What we have listed here is by no means the definitive list, but rather an edited selection of the vast array of imagery that can be sourced from the wonderful thing that is the Net. Just remember that not all material is free, so please respect the rules of copyright and take care to check before you use any images in your own design projects.

Some of the sites we've listed here are commercial image libraries that offer digital images at various sizes and at reasonable cost, while others offer images that are in the public domain and may, therefore, be free for you to use as you wish. It is your own responsibility to check carefully for licencing restrictions attached to any images that you choose to download from either the sites listed, or from any other sites you come across during the course of your research.

All of the sites we've listed are fully active at the time of this book's publication, but the Net is everchanging, and websites come and go. If any of the listed links are broken when you attempt to access them, we suggest you search for the name of the company or individual behind the site before giving up on the resource altogether as a small change in the URL may be all that is needed to gain access.

Free or not free?

Classing an image as being in the "public domain" might mean that it is free of charge, but not necessarily that it is free for you to use as you wish. Certain copyright restrictions may well exist for individual images, such as where the image can and can't be used, so please take every possible care when using images that you have found on the Net. Pages 038–039 cover Copyright and Creative Commons licencing in more detail.

Directory

123 RF
www.123rf.com
Over 3.3 million low-cost, royalty free images with a range of introductory offers. The high-quality images are mainly in the stock photo style with a broad range of subjects; some good clip-art graphics are also available.

All Free Backgrounds
www.allfreebackgrounds.com
Free downloadable backgrounds and graphics usable in both web and print projects.

Amazing Textures

amazingtextures.com

A texture library with hundreds of free and public domain textures, including high-resolution images suitable for print projects.

Backgrounds Archive

backgroundsarchive.com

A site offering thousands of free tileable background images organized by general subject category.

Burning Well

www.burningwell.org

Well worth a look despite it being a slightly hit-and-miss browsing experience. The images are public domain and largely donated by contributors to the site, but it may well be the place to find just what your after.

Coolclips

www.coolclips.com

A fairly extensive collection of free and royalty free cartoon-style clip-art which may suit projects and presentations that require a lighthearted look. Choose carefully as some of the material available will not look overly professional in use, but certain projects demand that kind of visual approach.

Corbis

pro.corbis.com

One of the big players in terms of commercial online image libraries, focusing on top-quality photography and covering all areas. The fees for the rights-managed images are high, but so is the quality of the material. A large number of royalty free images of equally high quality are also available at a more reasonable cost level.

Digital Vector Maps

digital-vector-maps.com

Royalty free and fully editable vector-based maps available at reasonable cost. You'll need software such as Adobe Illustrator if you want to edit the material in any way. The maps are also available as PDF files.

Dover Books

www.doverbooks.co.uk
store.doverpublications.com

Dover Books are a book publisher specializing in print-based clip-art books, some of which contain all the imagery within on accompanying CD ROMs. Much of the published material consists of reprinted public-domain imagery from the nineteenth and early twentieth centuries, and the company's name is a byword for good-quality clip-art resources. Many professional designers use Dover Books content in their illustration work.

Edupics

www.edupics.com

The site, at first glance, appears to offer clip-art material geared mainly toward children, but dig a little deeper and you'll find that there is a great deal more on offer. The combination of free and royalty free material extends to some potentially very useful high-resolution line drawings covering everything from animals and the environment to art, buildings, and religion. A very useful resource if you spend time exploring the content.

flickr

www.flickr.com

Before we go any further with this description, it is important to point out that flickr is not an image library in the conventional sense. It is an online photographic community, the equivalent of YouTube, but for photographers. The images posted by the millions of people who use the site are protected largely by Creative Commons licences (*see* page 039) and are often available for use by others, but please be extra careful to check before using any imagery sourced on this site. The rules are set out very clearly in the relevant sections. Aside from the image resource aspect of this amazing site, a general browse of the vast array of material on show provides a great source for inspiration and ideas, and also an everchanging creative barometer of what is visually fashionable at any one time.

Getty Images

www.gettyimages.com

The other big player in terms of commercial online image libraries that we choose to mention here as quality is extremely high. Unfortunately that, of course, means fees for the rights-managed images are also high, but you certainly get what you pay for.

Getty offer rights-managed and royalty free images as one would expect, but they also have an in-between category which they call *rights ready*. This offers images of a quality normally associated with rights-managed material, but the pricing is based on a flat-fee model that makes purchasing images much simpler. Clear explanations of each category are available on the Getty website.

iStockphoto

www.iStockphoto.com

A huge collection—over 3 million in fact—of royalty free photographic images and clip-art, with prices starting surprisingly low for small images suitable for use in websites. iStockphoto is one of the oldest *microstock* image libraries selling low-cost images in this way, and is often my first port of call for royalty free material. Images are purchased using credits that can be bought and stored in your account. Recommended.

Karen's Whimsy

karenswhimsy.com/public-domain-images

This is a really useful site with an extensive selection of free and public-domain historical clip-art. They are from the collection of Californian artist Karen Hatzigeorgiou who states, "You are free to use them [the images] in your artistic endeavors, either privately or commercially. My only request is that you not sell or give away the images themselves, either individually or as a collection. I spend a lot of time searching for and buying the source material, scanning, fixing, and editing the images, and then putting them on the web. By respecting these simple terms of use, you allow me to continue providing wonderful artwork that would remain hidden between the covers of these books, decayed from age, or tossed into landfills." Please do observe Karen's requests if you use this extremely useful resource.

Morgue File

www.morguefile.com

An interestingly named site which doesn't, as you might first think, feature images of dead people. It is actually a completely free image library featuring a wide range of high-quality, high-resolution images. The site is dedicated to "the propagation of free thought and exchange" and is highly recommended. While they are free, the images are not public domain, and some of the contributors request that you provide feedback on their images.

Stock XCHNG

www.sxc.hu

A free and royalty free site with a huge collection of high-quality images. This site in particular is rated highly by professional designers and illustrators, and is another personal favorite of mine. As well as the standard photographic material there is a good range of abstract and conceptual material that you can locate through the search facility, but be creative and expansive with the key words you enter to be sure that you locate all images that fit the category you are interested in.

You have to register with the site before you can download any material, but this is both free and a trouble-free process. There are some restrictions that are important to note, so check the rules of use carefully. In particular, you cannot use images from this site for any resale items (such as mugs or T-shirts).

Index

Acknowledgments

I would first of all like to thank my coauthor Jane Waterhouse for creating such a great range of projects, and for sharing the design and layout workload with me. Authoring a book can be a solitary process at times, and it's so much better when there are two of you.

I would like to thank Rick Landers for his terrific illustrations, which formed such an important part of the overall style for our book's design; and for his enthusiasm and professionalism, which was such a help to me during the layout stages. Thanks also to Chris Rubino, Brendan Cahill, and Alan Snow, who kindly allowed us to reproduce their work to illustrate points in the text.

To April Sankey, Lindy Dunlop, and the rest of the team at RotoVision, a big thankyou for your support during the project and for once again giving me the opportunity to author a book about a subject I love so much. I would also like to acknowledge the continued support of my friends and family whose encouragement and "haven't you finished that book yet?" comments cheered me along so often during the writing.

Finally, I could never have completed this book without the endless patience, encouragement, and support that my wife gave so selflessly. Thanks Sarah, you make all the hard work worthwhile.

Tony Seddon

I'd like to thank all the people who contributed to this project in their own way. In particular, thanks to April for having faith, to Tony for his approachable words, to Lindy for her calm expertise, to Rick for his playful illustrations, and most importantly to my husband Matthew for everything.

Jane Waterhouse